BEFORE IT'S TOO LATE

BEFORE IT'S TOO LATE

by
David Jeremiah

THOMAS NELSON PUBLISHERS
Nashville · Camden · New York

Published in Nashville, Tennessee, by Thomas Nelson, Inc. and distributed in Canada by Lawson Falle, Ltd., Cambridge, Ontario.

Printed in the United States of America.

Unless otherwise indicated, Scripture quotations in this book are from the King James Version of the Bible.

Scripture quotations marked NASB are from the *New American Standard Bible,* © The Lockman Foundation 1960, 1962, 1963, 1968, 1971, 1972, 1973, 1975, and are used by permission.

The poem on page 14, "So Long as There Are Homes," is from *Light of the Years* by Grace Noll Crowell. Copyright 1936, by Harper & Row, Publishers, Inc.; renewed © 1964 by Grace Noll Crowell. Reprinted by permission of the publisher.

Library of Congress Cataloging in Publication Data

Jeremiah, David.
    Before it's too late.

    1. Family—Religious life. 2. Christian ethics—
Baptist authors. 3. Church and social problems—
United States. 4. United States—Moral conditions.
I. Title.
BV4526.2.J45   1982   239'.4   82-18891
ISBN 0-8407-5818-9

To my wife, Donna,
without whose encouragement
this project would never
have been completed.

CONTENTS

ACKNOWLEDGMENTS

MY GRATEFUL APPRECIATION to Sally Wolff and Barbara Strong for typing and retyping the manuscript, to Dr. Ken Nichols for constantly encouraging me, to Randy Rebold and Glenda Parker for protecting my study time, to Dr. Tim LaHaye for his gracious preface, to Congressman Dan Coats who not only believes in but courageously stands for these truths, and finally to Dick and Deanna Freeland who first listened to these messages and strongly encouraged me to publish them.

FOREWORD

ONE OF THE healthiest signs of our times is the number of books coming out on the family. For too long, family life was deteriorating rapidly in our country and hardly anyone was noticing. That is no longer true; it is now fashionable to write on the subject.

Unfortunately, many writers do not really know what the problems are. Consequently, their solutions are often not related to life in the real world.

Let's face it, raising a family is not as easy as it was when we were young. When my widowed mother raised me, she could send me out on the streets of Detroit and did not have to worry that our neighborhood culture would attack the values she taught me at home. She didn't have to fear my finding pornographic literature, drugs, or alcohol, or my being accosted by a homosexual or local prostitute. That luxury is no longer possible today. Our "secular society" has mounted the most aggressive attack on the home in the history of America, yet many don't even know their loved ones are in danger.

David Jeremiah knows. And he knows the answers to the problems. I think you will enjoy his book and profit from it. I certainly did. Like everything else he does, his writing is thorough, biblical, and practical. He has carefully researched the problems and offers timely solutions based on biblical principles for defending your family and loved ones from some of the inevitable attacks on them from every side.

For over 12 years, I have traveled America holding Family Life Seminars. During that time, I have concluded that David Paul Jeremiah is the sharpest under-40 minister I know. You can imagine my delight upon learning that the church I served in San Diego for 25 years, where I am still a member, called him as its senior pastor. He is having an outstanding ministry in the lives of the church's people and, through radio and television, in lives throughout the entire community.

The interesting and meaningful contents of this book will have a similar ministry to you.

Tim LaHaye
President
Family Life Seminars

INTRODUCTION

WHY WRITE ANOTHER book about the family and other national concerns? What more can be said that hasn't been said? As I have labored over this manuscript, I have asked myself that question many times. Before you take your time to read what I have written, I owe you an answer.

I think this book may have been born in my mind as far back as 1976, at our Bicentennial. Perhaps for the first time, during those days I became aware of our spiritual heritage as a nation. The patriotic programs and "I Love America" concerts that toured our land during that celebration all seemed to be reminding us that the foundation of our nation was unique.

About that time, someone gave me a copy of Peter Marshall's, *The Light and the Glory*. I couldn't agree with everything I read in that book, but there was also much I couldn't deny. It was very obvious to me that God had blessed this young nation out of proportion to the other nations of the world. There just was no other explanation for America's dynamic two-hundred-year history.

One of the alarming side effects of my study of our American heritage was the realization that many of the characteristics of greatness that our nation embodied during the formative years were disappearing, and in their place the signs of deterioration and decay were multiplying.

I remember seeing a sign in the back window of an automobile that asked this question: "Can God bless a nation that kills its babies?" That question haunted me as I read the reports of the growing number of abortions in our land.

It was during the next few months that political action groups such as Moral Majority began to spring up nationwide. Many of the prime movers in these organizations were close friends of mine, and, consequently, I was constantly being asked my opinion of the role of the church in the political arena.

I found that question hard to answer. While on the one hand I agreed that our involvement in the political process was vital, I wasn't so certain that as a pastor I should merge my political and spiritual endeavors.

In my determination to be biblical, I decided I would limit my preaching to those issues the Bible addresses specifically. I began to make a list and to my amazement, I discovered that very few of the present issues facing the family and the nation were passed over in the Word of God. I started to prepare a series of messages on the subject "The Issues of the Eighties." During the summer of 1980, I preached that series to the wonderful people of the Blackhawk Baptist Church in Fort Wayne, Indiana. Those messages were the springboard for this book. The response from the church as well as the radio and television audiences encouraged me to continue my study.

Because of my outspoken stance on the issues addressed in this book, I have been asked more than once if I thought a person could be a Christian without being a political conservative. I have consistently answered that inquiry with the response that one's political persuasion has nothing to do with his or her personal salvation.

But I have also been careful to point out that some issues that have been considered political in nature are nothing more than biblical issues that have been dragged into the political arena. Abortion, pornography, homosexuality, morality, and the sanctity of the family are not matters to be decided by virtue of one's political affiliation. God had already voted on this agenda, and He has clearly instructed the believer to follow His example.

I hope you will read the twelve chapters of this book with concern. These are the issues of the eighties. Armed with the truth, we must act, before it's too late!

David Jeremiah
June 1982

SECTION I:
THE
HOME

CHAPTER
ONE

So Long as We Have Homes

So long as we have homes to which men turn
  at the close of day,

So long as we have homes where children are
  and women stay,

If love and loyalty and faith be found
  across these sills,

A stricken nation can recover from
  its gravest ills,

So long as we have homes where fires burn
  and there is bread,

So long as we have homes where lamps are lit
  and prayers are said,

Although a people falter through the dark
  and nations grope,

With God, Himself, back of these little homes
  we still have hope.

Grace Noll Crowell[1]

IS THE TRADITIONAL FAMILY OBSOLETE?

DR. HAROLD MOSER VOTH is a psychoanalyst and psychiatrist at the Menninger Clinic of Topeka, Kansas. He has written a book whose title seems almost vulgar. The book, *The Castrated Family*, cites the attacks against the traditional family that have surfaced during our generation. In his introduction, he summarizes the various forces that have been at work creating the present climate:

> The past twenty years have amply underscored the concept and predictions of future shock; indeed, the rapidity of social change, the revision and jettisoning of traditional folkways and social institutions, legislative and judicial efforts to promote major alterations in individual and social behavior have left the public with a pervasive sense of personal dislocation with perplexity and depression in their wake. We are daily treated to the erosion of traditional individual, familial, social, and religious values and ethics. Within this context the unusual becomes usual; the strange becomes familiar; the bizarre becomes commonplace; the perverse becomes the norm. God is dead, or demythologized or has undergone a change in sex; schools do not impart disciplined cognitive skills, but rather train the young to "adjust" to an increasingly confusing and polymorphous society; "equality" is legislated and adjudicated at the expense of individuality; there is no such thing as mental illness; legitimate authority is denigrated, even scourged; alcohol and drugs abound; crime continues to rise while divorce becomes commonplace and families disintegrate, leaving children in increasing numbers bereft of healthy parenting; illegitimate pregnancies burgeon in number, while abortion is just around the corner for any and all and the "pill" replaces individual responsibility for the conduct and issue of one's actions; civil rights zealots cloak their cruelty behind a facade of social con-

cern, while assorted "queens," lesbians, fetishists, sado-masochists and other sexual unfortunates find new forums for the popularization of their illnesses while they clamor that theirs is either the right way of at least no worse than anyone else's.[2]

Voth paints a very dark picture of the context in which the traditional family must survive.

According to Congressman Paul Weyrich, this onslaught against the family is nothing more than the:

> age-old conflict between good and evil . . . an attempt to keep souls from reaching eternal salvation. Among the anti-family forces are hardcore socialists who see it as a means by which they can obtain greater state control. One of the communists' chief objectives has always been to break down the traditional family . . . there is also a group of economic opportunists who profit by the decline of traditional values through pornography, abortion clinics, the contraceptive mentality and drug sales.[3]

Before we explore the various forces that are affecting the family within our culture, we do well to define our terms. Just what is a family—better yet, a "traditional" family?

During the 1980 "White House Conference on Families," organizers tried to avoid defining the family "in order to avoid [advocating] one particular form of the family over another."[4] Rhoda Glickman, one of the organizers, said, "Families are changing and adapting and there's nothing that's going to change that process. That's why we changed the name from White House Conference on the Family to White House Conference on Families—to show the diversity."[5]

Jim Guy Tucker, a liberal who was elected chairman of the White House Conference, gave leadership from the following perspective: to him, extremists were "the kind of people who display an aversion to abortion, the Equal Rights Amendment, feminism, contraceptives for teenagers and sex education in the schools." We should not be surprised that, with his outlook on life, he defines the family as "one or more adults living together with or without children."[6]

Other equally blurred and bad definitions come from *The American Home Economics Association:* "A family is two or three people who reside under the same roof and have a commitment to the future."[7] According to Richard J. Newhaus, Lutheran author and pastor, "Foster parents, lesbians and gays, liberated families or whatever—all can do the job as long as they provide children the loving and permanent structure that traditional families have typically provided."[8]

Jo Ann Casper, editor of a congressional newsletter for women and families, defines a family as, "persons who are related by blood, marriage, or adoption with a male father and a female mother."[9] Included in her definition is the idea that a single woman with children could be considered a family. This is the traditional and biblical definition (see Gen. 1:28, 2:24; Col. 3:18-21). The Pro-family Coalition uses this definition.

There is ample evidence to indicate that the foundation of our nation, our individual homes, is being eroded. Let me suggest ten major factors that contribute to that erosion.

1. THE DISAPPEARANCE OF THE RURAL LIFESTYLE

In his book *The Third Wave*, Alvin Toffler relates this apocryphal story. An executive decides to bring his son to his office one day and take him to lunch. The boy sees the plushly carpeted office, the indirect lighting, the elegant reception room. He sees the fancy expense account restaurant with its obsequious waiters and exorbitant prices. Finally, picturing their home and unable to restrain himself, the boy blurts out: "Daddy, how come you're so rich and we're so poor?"[10] The story illustrates the vocational credibility gap that exists today between parents and children; most children have absolutely no idea what their parents do for a living.

It has not always been this way. During the agricultural age, the family lived and worked together. The extended family consisted of parents and children living together within the same environment with grandparents and other relatives. The children grew with the various family roles being modeled and supported in every area of life. While living together, working together, and playing together, these families developed relationships of strength and vitality. They were the centers of life within the community.

O. R. Johnston, in *Who Needs the Family?*, points out that

the preindustrial family was a type of microcosm, undertaking for itself most of the tasks that the group needed to survive. Those various tasks he listed as follows:

> *Firstly,* the family regulated sexual expression and satisfaction, thus preventing constant conflict, confusion and competition. *Secondly,* the family regulated the production of children, thus ensuring that the community continued. *Thirdly,* the family socialized the children, transmitting the culture, and ensuring that they became mature citizens at some point in the future, to enter fully into the productive and continuing life of the society. *Fourthly,* the family protected the children. This protective function was in most cases undertaken not only in relation to the children but also to their grandparents; the active adults in most societies have not only handed duties down to their children, but also upwards to their elderly parents. *Fifthly,* after protection comes simple economic division of labor. This is seen in most primitive societies, whether they are hunting societies or gathering societies. It is the father who hunts or gathers, and it is the mother who rears the children. And *sixthly,* the family provides other resources which we can lump together—health care, recreation, training for work, and initiating into religion and myth, lore and literature. All of these tasks, in earlier societies and in most primitive societies today, were and are undertaken by the family for itself.[11]

But America has changed from a rural to an urban society within the last century. "In the forty-nine years, from 1920 through 1968, the total population of the United States nearly doubled; during the same interval the number of people on farms shrank by two-thirds, with the consequence that the farm population diminished proportionally from 30% of the total in 1920, to 5% in 1968."[12]

The broad generalization is at once obvious: In our transition from the rural, extended-family setting to the urban, nuclear-family setting, most of the functions once centered in the home have been institutionalized outside the home. There is nothing we can do about this development in society. We cannot go back and relive the transition, but we must understand the impact it has had on today's family. The centrifugal force of this revolution has decentralized the family and contributed greatly to our present-day breakdown.

2. THE DEREGULATION OF DIVORCE

Easy divorce is running wild in our land today. During the last decade, the rate of divorced persons per 1000 rose from 47 to 92—a 96 percent increase. Our church psychologist and I regularly counsel with people who are contemplating divorce. It has been easy to discern the developing trend. The threshold of divorce has gradually been lowered, even among Christian people.

The fallout from this explosion of divorce is far more extensive than most people realize. For instance, in Great Britain, where the divorce rate is just slightly ahead of our own, for every three divorces there are five children involved.[13]

This dimension of the broken family has created what Alvin Toffler calls the aggregate family. This term describes a family in which two divorced individuals with children marry each other, bringing the children of both marriages, and the adults as well, into a new, expanded family form. It is now estimated that 25 percent of American children are, or soon will be, members of such a family unit.[14]

According to Davidyne Mayleas, such units, with their "poly-parents," may be the mainstream family form of tomorrow. "We're into economic polygamy," says Mayleas, meaning that the two merged family units typically transfer money back and forth in the form of child support or other payments. The spread of this family form, she reports, has been accompanied by a rising incidence of sexual relations between parents and non-blood-related children.[15]

When three psychiatrists—Kellam, Ensminger, and Turner—attempted to map the "variations of families" found in a single poor, black neighborhood in Chicago, they identified no less than eighty-six different combinations of adults, including numerous forms of "mother-grandmother" families, "mother-aunt" families, "mother-stepfather" families, and "mother-other" families.[16]

The family structure that has been the stability of this land for over two hundred years is slowly disintegrating. Divorce for any cause is at the wheel of this downhill journey. One of the reasons for the continued growth in divorce figures is the apparent apathy with which modern man views the dissolution of a marriage. Even church people have been desensitized. More and more Christians are marrying for as long as they both shall love, instead of as long as they both shall live.

Recently, the United Methodist Church issued a new handbook of religious rituals, *Ritual in a New Day: An Invitation*. It thus distinguished itself as the first denomination in the nation to suggest formal observances of divorce in church. Part of the ceremony reads as follows:

> Dearly beloved, we have gathered here to solemnize the end of one time in Matthew and Anne's lives, and the beginning of another. "Matthew Surrey, do you now relinquish your status as husband for Anne, freeing her from all claims upon and responsibility to you except those that you willingly give to all other children of God?" (Matthew responds, "I do.") "Matthew, what sign do you give to Anne as a token of your forgiveness and your release to her?" He answers: "Her wedding ring reconsecrated to her freedom," placing the ring on the third finger of her right hand.[17]

The Task Force on the Cultural Context of Ritual, in the book's chapter on "Divorce Rituals," writes:

> At precisely the time when individuals are most lonely and need to establish links of communication with others, members of the Christian community know least how to respond . . . because the church plays a significant part in the initiation of a human relationship, so too, it ought to play a significant part in the termination of it . . . the church's attention to "the death of a marriage" is just as appropriate as "the necessary grief work" following the death of a loved one.[18]

No one denies the need to minister to those hurt by divorce, but to intimate God's blessing upon such action by solemnizing it in the church, before a pastor with a ritual, is to destroy one last fiber that binds marriages together. If the *church* so legitimizes divorce, who is left to represent God's standard?

3. THE DYNAMIC SINGLES EXPLOSION

Between 1970 and 1978, the number of persons aged 14 to 34 who lived alone nearly tripled in the United States, from 1.5

million to 4.3 million. Today, one-fifth of all households in the United States consist of a person living solo. A staggering one in seven American children are raised by a single parent, and in urban areas the number is one in four. The real estate industry has come up with "singles only" condominiums and has begun to respond to a need for smaller apartments and suburban homes with fewer bedrooms. Almost a fifth of all home buyers in the United States today are single.

If we include all the different kinds of single living in our country today, we must acknowledge that there are 50 million single people in our cities and suburbs. It has been estimated that they have a purchasing power of over 40 billion dollars.

The need for satisfying relationships among singles has stimulated a flock of new enterprises in recent years, including singles' bars, encounter groups, and computerized dating services. Even the Christian community has gotten into the act. An ad in a Christian magazine assured single Christians that "God did not ordain loneliness" and urged them to subscribe to a monthly publication through which they could supposedly get to "know other single Christians on four continents."

4. THE DISREGARD FOR THE MARRIAGE CEREMONY

The growth in the number of people who are living together without the legal formalities is astounding. The number has doubled in the last decade to a total of 1.3 million, according to authorities. The difficulty in assessing the extent of the problem ought to be obvious. However, the *open* declaration of live-in couples has become so common that the United States Department of Housing and Urban Development has changed its rules to permit such couples to occupy public housing. The courts throughout our land are wrestling with the legal and property complications that arise when such "non-marriage" couples "divorce." Hollywood stars such as Lee Marvin are leading the way in this new "marriageless marriage" trend.

Etiquette columnists write about which names to use in addressing partners, and "couple counseling" has sprouted as a new professional service alongside marriage counseling. These "marriages," besides violating God's law, are destroying the security of commitment that is necessary for rearing children with a strong self-image and a sense of worth.

5. THE DEVELOPMENT OF THE EQUAL RIGHTS AMENDMENT

The United States has just concluded one of the bitterest debates since the abolition of slavery with the consideration of the Equal Rights Amendment (ERA). If the ERA promoters had achieved their goal, they would have succeeded in tearing down the time-honored male and female role models that are necessary for the preservation of our society.

One does not have to do much research in the literature of the ERA exponents to discover their anti-God and anti-family determinations. Gloria Steinem, editor of *Ms. Magazine,* has written of her goal in the feminist battle: "By the year 2000, we will, I hope, raise our children to believe in human potential, not God." In a speech in Houston, Texas, Steinem said, "For the sake of those who wish to live in equal partnership, we have to abolish and reform the institution of marriage."[19]

Dr. Mary Jo Bane, associate director of Wellesley College's Center for Research on Women, wrote:

> We really don't know how to raise our children . . . the fact that children are raised in families means there's no equality . .   in order to raise children with equality, we must take them away from families who raise them.[20]

Perhaps the most frightening of all the statements by feminists is this paragraph from a paper called the *The Document: Declaration of Feminism*, by Nancy Lehmann and Helen Sullinger:

> Marriage has existed for the benefit of men and has been a legally sanctioned method of control over women . . . the end of the institution of marriage is a necessary condition for the liberation of women. Therefore, it is important for us to encourage women to leave their husbands and not to live individually with men . . . we must work to destroy marriage.[21]

With the end of marriage, called for by the feminists, there will be the necessary redefinition of the family. *The Document* states:

The nuclear family must be replaced with a new form of family where individuals live and work together to help meet the needs of all people in the society . . . with the destruction of the nuclear family must come a new way of looking at children. They must be seen as the responsibility of the entire society rather than individual parents.[22]

According to Dr. Jerry Falwell, there are five principles, or goals, that stand behind the major feminist movements in our country. They are as follows:
1. Man is the enemy.
2. Babies lead to bondage.
3. Total equality is a fact, not simply a goal.
4. Marriage must be eliminated.
5. *Above all,* religious belief must be changed.[23]

Dr. Voth has certainly touched the core of the matter when he describes the women's liberation movement as "that which, under the color of a compassionate concern for the selfhood of women, has cloaked a hatred and envy of males based upon a failure of maternal identification."[24]

6. THE DESENSITIZING EFFECT OF TV

The erosion of the American family has run a parallel course with the deterioration of TV standards. The "average" family on TV is no longer a nuclear family made up of a mother, father, and children. It consists of lesbians, homosexuals, divorced partners, and couples living together outside of wedlock.

The constant bombardment of Christian homes with the daytime soap operas explains much of the current family breakdown in our Bible-believing churches. A history of this trend might help to open our eyes:

At the University of Pennsylvania recently some communications students piled into an auditorium to watch a show on the "desensitization of America." The presentation, put on by the J. Walter Thompson advertising firm with the help of slides, film clips, and a running commentary, was a shocking and mind-numbing capsule of media history. It made a stark point. Since the 1950's, when America reveled in nothing more wicked than Marilyn Monroe, swing music, Milton Berle, and cowboy movies, the communications media has gradually escalated the level of sex titillation, bizarre violence, and greedy commercialism until they now reek of hucksterism and human degradation. Americans, it seems, live in a world of erotic soap operas, disaster films, pornographic magazines, sexually explicit novels, mind-pounding rock music, midnight shows, and dirty humor. Even the national magazines and newspapers today permit barracks language not allowed 20 years ago. The J. Walter Thompson Company, the largest advertising firm in the world, put together its presentation in order to convince prospective clients, as well as media students and industry executives, that the time has come to reach for a social goal higher than mere profit.[25]

"Sensation has been piled on sensation to capture a jaded public," Arnold Grisman, executive vice-president of J. Walter Thompson told the students. "Today's violence is tomorrow's ho-hum. In area after area, we are losing our capacity for feeling, and we are badly in need of a reappraisal. It is time to cool it, to resensitize ourselves."[26]

7. THE DEFECTION OF THE AMERICAN FATHER

We were holding our first family-life conference at the Blackhawk Baptist Church in Indiana. We had just moved into our new convocation center. We were privileged to have as our seminar leaders Dr. James Dobson and Joyce Landorf. This was one of the last seminars conducted by Dr. Dobson before the growth of his writing and other ministries, coupled with his renewed commitment to his family, dictated a significant change in his life-style.

It was the opportunity of a lifetime for my wife and me to be the hosts of Jim and Shirley Dobson. After one of the evening sessions, we were driving them back to their motel. As we arrived at the motel, Dr. Dobson said something like this to me: "David, tomorrow I'm going to speak on the 'Executive Father and Overcommitment.' I usually like to warn the pastor before I do this session, since he normally is one of the worst offenders."

I'm sure I swallowed hard. He had my number, all right. I had been working sixteen to eighteen hour days and checking in on my family occasionally at mealtime. Suddenly, I came up with a brilliant idea that I thought was sure to get me off the hook. "Dr. Dobson," I said, "I look at your commitments and schedule and responsibilities. Certainly, you must have some secret that I haven't found. How do you do it?" I remember that Shirley giggled—in today's language, it was a "gotcha." Jim Dobson then confessed that he, too, struggled with the problem but was coming to the only logical conclusion, which was a reduction in his commitments that took him away from home.

If you've read his books, listened to his radio program, or seen his films, you know all about the decisions he made in favor of his home. Some of the information he discussed in our seminar later appeared in two of his books. I am convinced the above conclusion was pivotal in his life, and it has become so in mine. In the following quotation from one of his books, Dobson talks about the amount of time most fathers spend with their children.

The August, 1974, issue of *Scientific American* included an important article entitled, "The Origins of Alienation," by Urie Bronfenbrenner. Dr. Bronfenbrenner is, in my opinion, the foremost authority on child development in America today, and his views should be considered carefully. In this article, Dr. Bronfenbrenner discussed the deteriorating status of the American family and the forces which are weakening its cohesiveness. More specifically, he is concerned about the circumstances which are seriously undermining parental love and depriving children of the leadership and love they must have for survival.

One of those circumstances is widely known as the "rat race." Dr. Bronfenbrenner described the problem this way, "The demands of a job that claim mealtimes, evenings and weekends as well as days; the trips and moves necessary to get ahead or simply to hold one's own; the increasing time spent commuting, entertaining, going out, meeting social and community obligations . . . all of these produce a situation in which a child often spends more time with a passive babysitter than with a participating parent."

According to Dr. Bronfenbrenner, this rat race is particularly incompatible with fatherly responsibilities, as illustrated by a recent investigation which yielded startling results. A team of researchers wanted to learn how much time middle-class fathers spend playing and interacting with their small children. First, they asked a group of fathers to estimate the time spent with their one-year-old youngsters each day, and received an average reply of fifteen to twenty minutes. To verify these claims, the investigators attached microphones to the shirts of small children for the purpose of recording actual parental verbalization. The results of this study are shocking: The average amount of time spent by these middle-class fathers with their small children was thirty-seven seconds per day! Their direct interaction was limited to 2.7 encounters daily, lasting ten to fifteen seconds each! That, so it seems, represents the contribution of fatherhood for millions of America's children.

Let's compare the thirty-seven-second interchanges between fathers and small children with another statistic. The average pre-school child watches between 30 and 50 hours of television per week. (The figures vary from one study to another.) What an incredible picture is painted by those two statistics. During the formative years of life, when children are so vulnerable to their experiences, they're receiving thirty-seven seconds a day from their fathers and 30 or more hours a week from commercial television![27]

8. THE DETERMINED INTERFERENCE OF THE GOVERNMENT

More than ever before, the government of the United States is moving in on the home. Some of the evidences are seen in such programs as the International Year of the Child. Cynthia Miller, who attended the International Year of the Child conference held in Texas and sponsored by the Department of Health, Education, and Welfare (HEW), reported, "In one workshop all the leaders agreed that any parent who teaches a child about Jesus Christ or Christianity, without presenting other religions to the child, is indeed discriminating against the child by not allowing him to choose his own values."[28]

In half our states, including many in the "Bible Belt," a father must abandon the home before a family can receive any federal assistance. Few government policies could be more anti-Christian and do more to undermine family life.[29]

A look at the items on the agenda of the White House Conference on Families shows how far-reaching the government's concern goes. Among other things the list includes:

parent-child relationships, preparation for family life, handicapped in the family, housing, education, health, law, media impact, status of homemakers, income security, the work place, tax policies, drug and alcohol abuse, and aging.

In a book by Onalee McGraw, *The Family, Feminism, and the Therapeutic State,* some of the extremes to which the enemies of the family plan to go are spelled out. For instance, a high-ranking HEW official called for the licensing of parents. McGraw points out that things have already proceeded to such a point legally that a University of California Law School (Berkeley) professor could write on the question *Is the Family Unconstitutional?* To show what the courts have already done, Sweden is considering a law to permit children to divorce their parents, and a like judgment is being sought in American courts.[30]

With its demonstrated ineffectiveness to operate in its delegated arena, why should the bureaucracy be allowed to take over the family? As one woman recently said, "If the government wants to help, let them stop printing worthless money, driving inflation upward, and making it necessary for mothers who want to stay home to go out and work just to put bread on the table and keep a roof overhead."

9. THE DETERIORATION OF THE PUBLIC SCHOOLS

In *Schools On Fire,* John Barton and John Whitehead cite ten characteristics, listed below, of today's school-age culture. Since over 60 million of our young people spend nearly seven hours per day in the public classroom, the impact of school experiences must be great.

1. More than half of all serious crime (murder, rape, aggravated assault, robbery, burglary, larceny, and grand theft auto) is committed by youths between the ages of ten and seventeen.
2. Over $600 million a year is being spent to repair damage done to school property by students; consequently, many school districts now spend more money annually on vandalism repair than they do on textbooks.
3. According to surveys published by the Department of

Health, Education, and Welfare, nearly half of all unmarried girls have intercourse before graduation from high school; the corresponding figure for unmarried boys is so close to 100% that statistics are no longer reported.

4. Just under 250,000 school-age girls give birth to babies each year; seen from another perspective, one out of every ten girls will give birth before reaching the age of eighteen.
5. The number of teenagers having abortions has climbed to an annual average of over 300,000.
6. The incidence of venereal disease among teenagers has reached "epidemic proportions."
7. Drug usage is now a critical problem at both the secondary and elementary levels of education; thousands of students in grade school "OD" each year (frequently while attending school), and many of these cases end in death.
8. Teenagers now rank second in incidence of alcoholism.
9. Next to accidents, suicide is now the leading cause of death among teenagers.
10. Scores at all levels of basic skills have steadily declined among high school students every year since 1963. Consequently, nearly one out of three adults whom our public schools now "graduate" into society is functionally illiterate.[31]

The symptoms tell the story of a deeper sickness. We have tried to educate our children in a moral vacuum, and we have failed miserably. The failure is so significant that it has helped produce 1500 Christian schools in our country. These schools are growing at the rate of three per day, and some experts are predicting that by 1990, there will be more students in Christian schools than in public schools.

Commenting on the Supreme Court decision of 1963 banning compulsory prayer and Bible reading in the public classroom, Dr. George Sweeting of Moody Bible Institute says that "the most serious effect of the decision is not that it cuts off children from prayer and Bible reading . . . but that it shouts that faith in God and reliance on the Bible are add-ons in the process of education . . . that God and faith have no place in education."[32]

Back in the sixteenth century, Martin Luther said, "I am much afraid that schools will prove to be the great gates of hell unless they diligently labor in explaining the Holy Scriptures, engraving them in the hearts of youth. I advise no one to place his child where the Scriptures do not reign paramount. Every institution where men are not unceasingly occupied with the Word of God must become corrupt."

Luther's prophecy has proved true. It is so sad to see Christian parents failing with their children while at the same time refusing the Christian school alternative. What parent, no matter how mature spiritually, can offset the influence of humanism and peer pressure exerted by the public schools for seven hours per day?

On June 28, 1971, the Supreme Court ruled that all education was to be divided into secular and sacred. But the notion that "secular" education is devoid of religious values is a myth. John Blanchard asserts,

> Secular education has its faith and its values, and these have a decided religious impact. The Supreme Court itself has said that the faith that there is no Supreme Being constitutes a religious conviction, and is to be respected as such. Secular education affirms in faith that "in the beginning was chance," that man is an animal, that truth is relative, and that death is the end. These are all articles of faith. Teaching of these articles of faith constitutes an establishment of religion. The use of tax money to support this significantly assails the constitutional rights of Bible-believing citizens. The constitutional rights of a significant number of citizens are being significantly assailed.[33]

Sadly, the dream of empty jails and prisons through public education has turned into the nightmare of violence in the public schools themselves.

10. THE DISCRIMINATION AGAINST THE UNBORN

Besides violating the prohibition against murder, the pro-abortion movement violates the right to life of an unborn child, deprecates the value of life itself, makes cheap the greatest gift of God to man apart from salvation, and opens the door to throwing away life at the other end of the life cycle as well.

When I began this study, I had the opportunity of discussing a synopsis of these messages with our "Super Sixties" senior citizens group. When I said I was going to preach a message on the subject of abortion, I asked those gray-haired people if anybody in a group like theirs would be interested in that subject. One of the men raised his hand and said, "Pastor, we *are* interested in abortion, because we realize that if abortion is legalized, the next thing that will be approved in our country is euthanasia." Anything that degrades life is in opposition to the Word of God. The pro-abortion movement has caused promiscuity to explode in our country, because now there is no longer any fear of illegitimate pregnancy. Just throw the baby away and go on.

Whatever cheapens life erodes the fiber of the family and degrades the personal dignity of the individual. It is no wonder our self-respect and self-esteem are at an all-time low. If life is so cheap as to be disregarded at a whim, what is there really to live for?

These ten factors that contribute to the erosion of the home are by no means the only forces at work. Some of the other influences, such as pornography and homosexuality, are discussed fully elsewhere in this book.

These are the characteristics of today. What of tomorrow? What kind of family model will our children see when they are ready to marry? Family therapist Virginia Satir, in a book entitled *Peoplemaking,* paints this picture of the future family:

> What if all the practices now going on, which we have labeled as morally bad, were instead really evidence of the great variations in human beings? In the case of the many-times-married person, perhaps, there are some people whose level of interest is short and so they choose one mate after another. Instead of considering this a short-coming, what would happen if we treated this as a simple variation? Such people could enter a limited marriage contract, say from one to five years. If the contract were not renewed at its end, then the dissolution of the marriage could take place. Perhaps the married people who have heterosexual

relationships outside marriage are not simply "adulterers," but are people with a human need. After all, polyandry and polygamy were once respected forms of marriage. And why not have a group of communal marriage? When you think about it, marriage merely legalizes a relationship between a male and female adult that entitles them to certain property and a certain guarantee against exploitation. Why does it have to be limited to just one man and one woman? If we fully trusted one another and were truly responsible, we would not be exploitive and we could share fairly.[34]

Is the traditional family obsolete? If the answer is derived from a consensus of sociologists and futurists, there is no future for the family in its present form.

But we can be a part of a better answer. To use a well-worn phrase, we are either contributing to the solution or we are a part of the problem.

Courageously evaluate your role as parents as you reflect upon these ten questions:

1. Do we perceive ourselves as being an important part of the battle for the family? The family is a battleground today because too many good people thought it was someone else's job to care.

2. Do we portray the biblical roles of marriage before our children? Feminism and homosexuality are usually just one generation removed from the homes where the biblical roles are reversed.

3. Do we participate actively in the political process by supporting those candidates who stand for the family, not only with their speeches but also with their votes?

4. Do we protest against the government's interference in our home, or are we passively allowing it to take over our families?

5. Do we profess to be educating our children God's way while giving them to secular public schools for the best seven hours of their day? How far would you drive and how much would you pay if you knew it would save the lives of your children?

6. Do we plan time together as a family? How many minutes did *you* spend with your children today?

7. Do we preach the value and dignity of human life? Our

respect for the elderly and our hatred for abortion must not be kept secret from our children.

8. Do we preview the television programs that are watched in our home? Most Christian parents consider a program acceptable if it does not include obscene language. Far more dangerous than profanity, however, is the communication of the world's life-style, including divorce, promiscuity, homosexuality, abortion, and so on.

9. Do we pray for the future marriages of our children? I was recently in the home of a pastor friend and heard him pray out loud for his teenage children who were sitting there beside him. He prayed, "O Lord, keep my children from divorce." You may consider that to be negative praying, but before throwing the idea away, why not read today's divorce suit statistics in your newspaper?

10. Do we practice what we claim to believe? Studies show that the number one reason why children reject their parents' values is the inconsistent lives of the parents.

NOTES

1. Grace Noll Crowell, *Light of the Years* (New York: Harper and Row, 1936).
2. Harold M. Voth, *The Castrated Family* (Kansas City, KS: Sheed Andrews & McMeel, 1977), p. VII, VIII.
3. Paul Weyrich, *Conservative Digest*, May/June 1980, p. 12.
4. John Maust, "The White House Feud on the Family," *Christianity Today*, May 2, 1980, p. 47.
5. Ibid., p. 48.
6. Ibid. pp. 48–49.
7. Bob Whitmore, "The White House Conference on Families: How It May Affect Your Home," *Faith for the Family*, July/August 1980, p. 6.
8. Ibid.
9. Ibid.

10. Alvin Toffler, *The Third Wave* (New York: William Morrow, 1980), p. 236.
11. O. R. Johnston, *Who Needs the Family?* (Downers Grove, IL: InterVarsity, 1979), pp. 16, 17.
12. Robert F. Winch, *The Modern Family* (New York: Holt, Rinehart and Winston, 1971), p. 86.
13. O. R. Johnston, *Who Needs the Family?* p. 119.
14. Alvin Toffler, *The Third Wave*, p. 231.
15. Ibid.
16. Ibid.
17. *Ritual in a New Day: An Invitation* (Nashville: Abingdon, 1976).
18. Ibid.
19. Quoted by Jerry Falwell, *Listen America* (Garden City, N.Y.: Doubleday, 1980), p. 153.
20. Ibid.
21. Nancy Lehmann & Helen Sullinger, *The Document: Declaration of Feminism*. Quoted in *Listen America*, p. 153.
22. Ibid.
23. Ibid.
24. Harold M. Voth, *The Castrated Family*, p. VIII.
25. Saikowski, Charlotte, "TV's Problem: Can Decency Be Made to Pay?" *The Christian Science Monitor*, April 14, 1976.
26. Ibid.
27. James C. Dobson, *Straight Talk to Men and Their Wives* (Waco, TX: Word, 1980), pp. 35, 36.
28. Rosemary Thompson, "A National Policy on Family Life: Making Your Voice Heard," *Christian Life*, February 1980.
29. Ibid.
30. Onalee McGraw, *The Family, Feminism, and the Therapeutic State* (Washington, D.C.: Heritage Foundation), pp. 21, 41, 65.
31. John Barton and John Whitehead, *Schools on Fire* (Wheaton, IL: Tyndale, 1980), pp. 9-10.
32. George Sweeting, *Special Sermons on Special Issues* (Chicago: Moody, 1981), p. 59.
33. John F. Blanchard, Jr., "Can We Live with Public Education?" *Moody Monthly*, October 1971, p. 89.
34. Quoted by O. R. Johnston, *Who Needs the Family?* p. 126.

CHAPTER
TWO

I Walked Today

I walked today as Dante walked
In days of long ago;
I gasped through stench of this earth's hell;
The air was filled with woe.
Men scarred with sin, in rags, ill shod,
   Their faces blank in despair,
   Their livid eyes burned into me—
   My joy turned into misery.
   I cried, "O Christ of Calvary,
Awake Thy church to care!"

I walked today where Christ would walk
If He were here on earth;
The air was thick with discontent
And total lack of mirth.
   It seemed despair had carved each face;
   And greed and lust and vice,
   Like chains, had bound resentful men.
   "And, Lord," I asked, "Oh when, oh when
   Will Thy dear church revive again
To seek Thy power in prayer?"

I walked today mid cultured vice,
And as I walked, I wept.
I thought, Lord, of Thy sacrifice
And how Thy church has crept
   Along the road this past decade
   And slumbered in soft pews,
   While millions in their sinful plight
   Fall into hell's eternal night.
   O Christ, in mercy purge our blight;
Anoint Thy church to tell!

Leonard Ravenhill

IS HOMOSEXUALITY AN ALTERNATE LIFESTYLE?

HOMOSEXUALITY IS ALMOST as old as man. The first mention of it in recorded history concerns Lot and the well-known cities of Sodom and Gomorrah, over four thousand years ago. The word *sodomy,* copulation with a member of the same sex, has become a byword for homosexuality and is obviously derived from that ancient city. Certainly there have been homosexuals in America since the early days of our country, but the militant and open flaunting of homosexual perversion is a relatively recent development.

The homosexual revolution in our country began, according to most experts, in the summer of 1969, in Manhattan's Greenwich Village. Four hundred gays flooded the streets for several nights to protest police raids on the Stonewall Inn, a homosexual bar on Christopher Street. The anti-Viet Nam, civil rights, and women's rights movements all helped galvanize the gays into thinking that they, too, could make a claim on society for recognition of their basic rights and point of view. From that date until the present, the gays have been on the march, making inroads into almost every segment of society. The following are just a few of the many advances of the Gay Rights Movement in our country today:

- Homosexual men and women are "coming out of the closet" as never before to live openly. They are colonizing areas of big cities as their own territory, operating bars and advertizing gay clubs in both large and small cities.
- The "Blueboy," a magazine something like a homosexual "Playboy," is published by Donald Embinder, a forty-four-year-old gay publisher. At the last check, the magazine had a circulation of over 135,000.

- According to the Institute of Sex Research founded by Kinsey, it is estimated that homosexuals constitute 10 percent of the United States population—13 percent of the males and 5 percent of the females. According to Kinsey, only 1 percent of them are out of the closet. The rest reveal their homosexuality only to themselves and perhaps a few trusted friends. (The Kinsey Reports that have been the source of most sexual information since 1948 must be viewed critically, as they are really more propaganda than scientific research. The Kinsey reports popularize and encourage promiscuity from an anti-God, anti-morality foundation.)
- Thirty-nine cities, towns and counties, including Detroit, Washington, D.C., and Minneapolis, have enacted ordinances forbidding discrimination against homosexuals in jobs and housing. To the credit of the opponents of the Gay Movement, only five of these have been added to the list in the past two years. In 1979, the Connecticut House of Representatives voted down a gay rights bill.
- In 1975, the Civil Service Commission, responding to a federal court decision, issued guidelines stating that people could not be denied federal employment solely because of homosexuality. The FBI and the CIA are still holding out, and the Defense Department clings to a hard-line policy: "Known homosexuals are separated from military service."
- One hundred twenty major national corporations, including AT&T and IBM, have announced that they do not discriminate in hiring or promoting people because they are homosexuals.
- TV and movies are treating gay themes more openly and sympathetically. ABC's hit series "Soap," for example, had two homosexual characters, one a macho football player.
- The Harvard Law School will not allow any law firms that discriminate against homosexuals to use its placement service for employment interviews.
- In San Francisco, where homosexuals are flocking by the

thousands from all over the country to Castro Street and Haight-Ashbury, gays are being recruited for the police department.

- Today, Washington, D.C. has over eighty homosexual organizations, and Boston, with seventy, even has a club for overweight lesbians.
- In Boston, the Homophile Community Health Service provides psychological counseling for gays who fear that straight doctors will tell them that the source of all their problems is their homosexuality.
- The Metropolitan Community Church, largely made up of homosexuals, is headquartered in Los Angeles and has 110 congregations and mission stations. It even sends out missionaries to organize new churches throughout the U.S., Canada, and Europe.
- Gay rights legislation is being sought that would elevate homosexuality to normalcy along with heterosexuality, give gays increased leverage to secure jobs on a quota basis, force the military and public schools to hire avowed homosexuals, and make it impossible for even church organizations to fire a homosexual if he or she were discovered after hiring.
- The United Methodist Church's highest legal agency recently upheld the appointment of practicing homosexual Paul Abels as pastor of New York City's Washington Square Church.[1]

In light of the growth of this movement in our country, we do well to ask what the Creator thinks of these things. When God created the world, He established a fundamental distinction within the human race, reflected in the human body—"male and female created he them" (Gen. 1:27; 5:2). It was God's plan for sexual relations to be in the form of man-woman union, man and wife becoming "one flesh" (Gen. 2:24). The distinction between the sexes cannot be explained apart from that fact. God does not create man alone, neither does He create man/man or woman/woman. God creates man as male and female, and only in union together is the image of God seen upon the earth.

Homosexuals and their defenders, who argue that all human beings have the right to self-understanding and expression, reflect their determination to ignore God's design and replace His intended distinctions with their own desires.

Greg L. Bahnsen, in his book *Homosexuality—A Biblical View,* puts this into perspective:

> Because man's sexual identity is defined by God, because his orientation is ordained by God, and because his sexual activity is circumscribed within a heterosexual marriage context, homosexuality cannot be viewed merely as a variant sexual preference or accidental variation within creation (akin to left-handedness). It is not a third natural sex or alternative sexual orientation in God's diverse world. Instead, it represents a choice, in some sense, to set one's desires and satisfy one's physical drives in a way contrary to God's appointment and creation. There is no natural homosexuality, for homosexuality is precisely a perversion of nature (understood as God's design for human relations). Homosexuals are made, not born; their disorder is developed contrary to their god-given identity, learned in opposition to the created order. Pursued in defiance of the marriage ordinance.[2]

The biblical account of Creation destroys the homosexual's defense. In light of God's Word in general and Genesis in particular, homosexuality is a severely perverted condition.

THE STORY OF SODOM

In the story of Sodom, the men of Sodom demanded that the two guests of Lot be brought out so that the Sodomites might "know" them (Gen. 19:5). The result of this activity by the citizens of Sodom was the smiting of the Sodomites with blindness. And the universal sinfulness of the city led to its destruction by fire and brimstone.

Ezekiel 16 mentions other sins besides homosexuality that made up the general wickedness of the city of Sodom (pride, fullness of bread, abundance of idleness, failure to help the poor and needy, haughtiness—see Ezek. 16:49-50).

But it was the "abomination" of homosexuality that caused the dire judgment of God (see Gen. 18:21 and 19:13). This was the mark of their extreme rebellion and degradation. For twenty centuries the church has maintained its position against homosexuality, as seen in the writings of Calvin, Luther, Barth, and, more recently, Bruce Metzger.

The advocates of "Christian homosexuality" wrest the Scriptures from their normal interpretation by making the sin of Sodom to be the sin of inhospitality. In 1955, Errick Bailey, an Anglican, defied the view of two millenia of orthodox consensus and said that "to know" meant "to get acquainted with." John J. McNeil, an avowed homosexual and a Catholic priest, popularized this view through his book *The Church and the Homosexual*. According to this theory, the Lord reduced Sodom to ash because of the lack of love and social courtesy.

This humanistic view of the incident will not stand the investigation of honest scholarship. First, Lot's response to their request argues against such a view. Lot answered their demand "to know" his guests by urging them not to act "so wickedly," and he slammed the door to keep the lusting inhabitants of Sodom from their prey (see Gen. 19:6-7).

Second, those who interpret "know" as "get acquainted with" cannot explain the very obvious use of the same word in the immediate context. Lot described his daughters as ones "who have not *known* man." Are we to assume that they had never "been acquainted" with man? Some homosexual interpreters explain Lot's offer of his daughters as "sexual bribery," but one cannot interpret *yada* metaphorically in verse 5 and change its meaning in verse 13.

Sodom was obliterated because it was a city full of homosexuals who day after day practiced their sensual abomination. Their homosexual sin, according to Paul, was "worthy of death" (Rom. 1:32).

The Bible leaves no doubt about the nature of their sin. Jude 7 declares that Sodom was destroyed for violating the ordinance of God in the distinction between men and women: "Even as Sodom and Gomorrah, and the cities about them in like manner, giving themselves over to fornication, and going after strange flesh, are set forth for an example, suffering the vengeance of eternal fire" (Jude 7).

The word translated "fornication" is *ekporneuein*. It is intensive, thus pointing to extravagant lust. The words "giving themselves over to" translate the word *apelthousai*, which means the absolute abandonment to impurity. The words "strange flesh" refer to unnatural sexual intercourse with "different flesh."

THE LAW OF GOD

Along with God's specific marriage ordinance detailing sexual differentiation and the record of the destruction of Sodom, we also have several clear statements in the Law of God as revealed in the Old Testament.

The seventh commandment protects sexual chastity and the integrity of the family. The further amplification of God's "Family Protection Act" is found in a number of other passages.[3] We are told in one of the passages that the integrity of the family is violated by homosexual behavior: "Thou shalt not lie with mankind, as with womankind: it is abomination" (Lev. 18:22). Verse 24 of the same chapter continues the thought: "Defile not ye yourselves in any of these things: for in all these the nations are defiled which I cast out before you." Verse 30 continues, "Therefore shall ye keep mine ordinance, that ye commit not any one of these abominable customs, which were committed before you, and that ye defile not yourselves therein: I am the LORD your God."

Leviticus 20:13 further underscores God's hatred for this sin: "If a man also lie with mankind, as he lieth with a woman, both of them have committed an abomination: they shall surely be put to death; their blood shall be upon them." From the Law of God, His verdict on homosexuality is inescapably clear.

Some argue that these statements from the Old Testament Law are not binding on us today. Recently, one of our young people gave me a tract that was distributed by the gay community on the Purdue University campus. The pamphlet, entitled "Homosexuality—What the Bible Does and Does Not Say," attempts to refute the biblical prohibitions against homosexuality.

In one section the pamphlet tries to deal with the passages we have just read in the following manner:

> Anyone who is concerned about this prohibition should read the whole chapter or the whole book of Leviticus: No pork, no lobster, no shrimp, no oysters . . . no eating blood, no rare meats, no interbreeding of cattle, and a whole host of other laws.[4]

The problem with such an "easy" answer is obvious to an honest student of the Bible. The ceremonial laws and the dietary laws mentioned in the above illustration have indeed been abrogated for the believer (see Matt. 15:10-19; Acts 10:9-16; Rom. 13:21; 14:1-4; Gal. 3:1-14; 5:1-12; Heb. 8-10). By the obedience of Christ in His redemptive work, all those Old Testament ceremonial laws have been completely fulfilled. They were the shadow of which Christ is the substance (see Heb. 10:1). Christ came and "taketh away the first, that he may establish the second" (Heb. 10:9). Every Bible student recognizes the category of temporary ceremonial law in the Old Testament (see Heb. 10:1-18).

But the sleight-of-hand trick by the homosexual exegetes is the assigning of homosexuality to the category of ceremonial law. Homosexuality does not picture the person and work of Christ in any sense. In Israel, it was punishable by death and, therefore, clearly categorized as a moral law; thus it was not temporary. The Bible never changes God's revealed moral law, but rather strongly reaffirms it in the New Testament—not as a way of being right with God, but as a declaration of God's unchanging and righteous will for His people.

Bahnsen summarizes the Old Testament information on homosexuality:

> God has created man in such a way and ordered social relations in such a way, God has worked such judgment in the course of history, God has such a Holy character as is transcribed in the law that homosexuality is "an abomination." It upsets the proper sexual relations between people, representing an attempt to redefine man and the world in the image of the sinner. It provokes the wrath of God, is diametrically opposed to His

nature, and is punishable by death. This much is taught in the creation account. The story of Sodom and the Law of God.[5]

THE GOSPELS

Sometimes it is argued that Jesus never mentioned homosexuality in the Gospels, and therefore it must be all right. The age-old argument that silence means consent can be mighty handy when one is on the wrong side of the truth. The fact is, however, that when Jesus spoke about human sexuality, He always presupposed heterosexuality. When He was teaching the meaning of the bill of divorce, He appealed to creation:

> Have ye not read, that he which made them at the beginning made them male and female, and said, For this cause, shall a man leave father and mother, and shall cleave to his wife: and they twain shall be one flesh? Wherefore they are no more twain, but one flesh. What therefore God hath joined together, let not man put asunder (Matt. 19:4-6).

ROMANS 1

The first chapter of Romans has been called the devolution of man by some. It contains the declaration of God's righteousness and pronounces God's wrath upon all who suppress the truth in unrighteousness.

Romans 1 is the most devastating passage in the Bible for practicing homosexuals. Here Paul teaches that the wrath of God is revealed from heaven against those who turn from their proper relationship to the Creator, holding down the truth of God, and practicing idolatry. Because they do this, says Paul, God gives them over to impure lusts, the dishonoring of their bodies. Men who give up God are given up by God to wander in moral pollution. That moral perversion called "homosexuality" is described in this passage by the following: "uncleanness, . . . to dishonor their own bodies" (1:24); "vile affections" (1:26); "indecent acts" (NASB) or "error" (1:27); "a depraved mind" (1:28 NASB); "change the natural use into that which is against nature" (1:26); and therefore, "worthy of death" (1:32).

According to Paul, homosexuality is the cultural culmination of rebellion against God. It is symptomatic of a society under judgment, inwardly corrupted to the point of collapse. Paul regarded it as the evidence of degeneracy that caused God in His wrath to give up the nations.

Even in the face of such clear evidence, gay apologists argue. Bailey and McNeil assert that Paul was condemning homosexual lust and promiscuity rather than homosexual acts. They also suggest that when Paul talked about "natural relations," he was referring to the individual person's natural affectional preference. Thus, in their view, if a homosexual was to do what was natural for him, he must love a person of the same sex. To do otherwise would be for him unnatural. One could not ask for a better illustration of Paul's assessment of gay theology—according to Romans 1:25, the basis of their thinking is a lie.

1 CORINTHIANS

"Do not be deceived; neither fornicators, nor idolaters, nor adulterers, . . . nor homosexuals . . . shall inherit the kingdom of God" (1 Cor. 6:9-10 NASB).

Here Paul uses two Greek words to refer to homosexuality: *malakio* and *arsenokoitai*. These two words were used consistently by Greek authors to apply to the full spectrum of homosexuality. Only the wildest of religious speculation can avoid the conclusion that Paul knew both exactly what he meant and how he would be understood when he used those terms.

1 TIMOTHY

Paul in 1 Timothy 1:8 repeats his theme from Romans that the Law is good if it is used to help us to recognize our sin and come to Christ for repentance. But he goes on to say that the Law is made for the:

lawless and rebellious, for the ungodly and sinners, for the unholy and profane, . . . immoral men and homosexuals and kidnappers and liars and perjurers, and whatever else is contrary to sound teaching (1 Tim. 1:9-10 NASB).

Here again is the same word as used in 1 Corinthians: *arsenokoitai,* which means "sodomite" or "homosexual." Again in this passage, the homosexual is in bad company.

Thus, as we examine Scripture, we discover that from Genesis to Leviticus, from the original Creation to the destruction of Sodom to the holy Law of God, the message is the same. From Christ's statement on marriage in the Gospels to Paul's clear statements against homosexuality in Romans, 1 Corinthians, and Timothy, we learn that God created man, male and female, and that they are to be fulfilled in faithful heterosexual relationships within marriage. It is the same for every culture, and it is binding on us today.

In light of the clear biblical information we have just examined, what should be our attitude and position today? Below are several mandates.

1. *We must refuse to allow the exponents of the gay movement to put us on the defensive.* It is the homosexual who has stepped out of the revealed will of God, not the heterosexual Christian. More than ever before, the moral Christian is being asked to defend himself against the unwarranted accusations of the homosexual. Someone has called their strategy "Rhetorical Terrorism." Two examples will illustrate their plan:

(A) *"To be against homosexuality is to demonstrate a lack of love."* C. S. Lewis once said, "To ask that God's love be content with us as we are is to ask that God should cease to be God: because He is what He is, His love must in the nature of things, be impeded and repelled by certain stains in our present character and because He already loves us He must labour to make us lovable."[6] Love is at stake here. We must choose either to love sin or love God. If we love God, we will keep His commandments.

(B) *"To judge a homosexual or his homosexuality is to be a bigot and thus displease the Lord."* Viewing something as immoral is not the same as being a bigot. Is it customary to look on someone who condemns the killing of innocent people as a bigot toward murderers?

2. *We must refrain from any attempt to reinterpret the biblical evidence in light of our present culture.* When our doctrine is adjusted by human wisdom or our examination of human behavior, we have destroyed the only authority God has given us to guide our lives. If it is possible to reinterpret Scripture to endorse homosexuality, we can make it endorse anything anyone would like to do or believe. It is important that we base our practice upon our doctrine and not our doctrine upon our practice. Our standards are defined by the Word of God. We can accept those standards or reject them, but we cannot tamper with them. What is at stake is not gay rights, but God's rights.

3. *We must reject totally the idea that one can be a Spirit-filled Christian and a practicing homosexual at the same time.* The biblical evidence will not allow that position. It is impossible to enter the Kingdom while rejecting and violating the standards of the King. We cannot maintain our Christian integrity if we condone what God condemns. To recognize a gay church as a church in the biblical sense of the word is to degrade the term "church." You might as well have churches for fornicators, adulterers, murderers, and robbers. The church is called to bring back the straying sheep. We are not called to say to the straying sheep that they are okay in their wanderings and that we ordain their devious paths as alternate lifestyles.

4. *We must resist as Christian citizens the attempts that are being made on the local and national levels to normalize or legalize homosexuality.* It is not possible to give the militant gays what they want without sentencing millions of youth to a lifetime of misery. This is a price too high to pay. It violates the moral standards of God, is destructive to our country, and is in opposition to the best interests of our youth. Dr. Charles W. Socarides, clinical professor of psychiatry at the State University of New York and a leading authority on the treatment of homosexuality, warned:

There's no doubt in my mind that if homosexuality is further normalized and raised to a level of complete social acceptability, there will be a tremendous rise in the incidence of homosexuality. It would have dire effects for society. Homosexuality militates against the family, drives the sexes in opposite directions and neglects the child's growth and sexual identity.[7]

5. *We must recognize the relationship between homosexuality and inadequate home life.* Dominant mothers and hostile or absentee fathers are creating a predisposition toward homosexuality. Dr. Irving Bieber studied the family backgrounds of 106 male homosexuals. According to his research, 81 mothers were dominating, 62 were overprotective, 66 made the homosexual their favorite child; 82 of the fathers spent very little time with their sons, and 79 fathers maintained a detached attitude toward them.[8] The best way to stamp out homosexuality, according to Dr. Tim LaHaye, is to get back to the business of making parenthood a priority. Children raised in loving, well-disciplined homes, where mother and father are good role models for their children, rarely become homosexual.[9]

6. *We must reach out compassionately to those who are struggling to be free of the sin of homosexuality.* Like Christ, we must have compassion on the sinner while at the same time we are condemning the sin. Dr. Melvin Anchell said that whoever decided to call homosexuals gay must have had a terrible sense of humor.[10] They are lonely, guilty, often depressed people. Their only hope is Jesus Christ, and we must be His caring ambassadors to them.

It is interesting to note that in the context of the three passages in which Paul addressed the subject of homosexuality, he held out the only hope of recovery for the homosexual as being in the person of the Lord Jesus Christ.

Romans 3:23-24. "For all have sinned, and come short of the glory of God; being justified freely by his grace through the redemption that is in Christ Jesus."

1 Corinthians 6:11. "And such were some of you: but ye are washed, but ye are sanctified, but ye are justified in the name of the Lord Jesus, and by the Spirit of our God."

1 Timothy 1:15. "This is a faithful saying, and worthy of all acceptation, that Christ Jesus came into the world to save sinners; of whom I am chief."

The hope of the homosexual today is the same as it was in Paul's day. Jesus Christ can and will wash away any sin. The sin of homosexuality is not a stain too deep to respond to the cleansing power of His blood.

NOTES

1. Much of this statistical information was reported in a special issue of *Time*, April 23, 1979.
2. Greg L. Bahnsen, *Homosexuality—A Biblical View* (Grand Rapids, MI: Baker, 1979), p. 30.
3. God's "Family Protection Act" includes prohibitions against seduction of a virgin (see Ex. 22:1); rape of an unbetrothed virgin (see Deut. 22:28); rape of a betrothed virgin (see Deut. 22:23-27); adultery with or rape of another's wife (see Lev. 20:10; Deut. 22:22); incest (see Lev. 20:11, 12, 14; Deut. 17, 20, 22, 23); bestiality (see Ex. 22:19; Lev. 18:23; 20:15, 16); homosexuality (see Lev. 18:22, 20:13).
4. *Homosexuality—What the Bible Does and Does Not Say.* A pamphlet published by the Universal Fellowship of Metropolitan Community Churches in Los Angeles, California. (The Metropolitan Community Churches are the gay churches of America.)
5. Greg L. Bahnsen, *Homosexuality—A Biblical View,* p. 47.
6. C. S. Lewis, *The Problem of Pain* (New York: Macmillan 1974), pp. 45–48.
7. *National Enquirer,* June 1977.
8. Irving Bieber, *Homosexuality, A Psychoanalytic Study of Male Homosexuals* (New York: Basic Books, 1962), n.p.
9. Tim LaHaye, *The Unhappy Gays* (Wheaton, IL: Tyndale, 1978), p. 75.
10. Murray Norris, *Christian Family Renewal Letter.*

CHAPTER
THREE

Ballad of the Unborn

My shining feet will never run
  On early morning lawn,
My feet were crushed before they
  Had a chance to streak the dawn.

My fingers now will never stretch
  To touch the winning tape,
My race was done before I learned
  The smallest steps to take.

My growing height will never be
  Recorded on the wall,
My growth was stopped when I was still
  Unseen and very small.

My lips and tongue will never taste
  The good fruit of the earth;
For I myself was judged to be
  A fruit of little worth.

My eyes will never scan the sky
  For my high flying kite;
For when still blind, destroyed were they
  In the black womb of night.

I'll never stand upon a hill
  Spring wind in my hair,
Aborted winds of thought closed in
  On motherhood's despair.

I'll never walk the shores of life
  Or know the tides of time;
For I was coming but unloved
  And that my only crime.

Author Unknown

IS ABORTION MURDER?

EVERY TWENTY-FOUR HOURS there are 3600 unborn American babies killed. That's 1.32 million per year, and it's all perfectly legal. This killing is called abortion, the expulsion of the human fetus prematurely (that is, before it is capable of surviving outside the womb). Accident may cause abortion, or artificial means may induce one. A *therapeutic* abortion is done when the termination of the pregnancy is necessary for the sake of the mother's physical health; a *psychiatric* abortion, for her mental health. *Eugenic* abortion is used as a means of keeping retarded or deformed children from being born; *social* abortion is used to ease economic pressure on a family; *ethical* abortion is used in cases of rape or incest; and *abortion on demand* permits abortion for any or no reason. *Spontaneous abortion,* over which no one has control, happens to about 30 percent of all fertilized eggs.[1]

The Supreme Court has ruled that abortion, even abortion on demand, is an American freedom. But we don't call it abortion anymore. We call it "post-conceptive fertility control." Feminists call it "voluntary miscarriage" and every woman's right. They say it makes every child a wanted child and lowers the incidence of child abuse. Pro-lifers call abortion "murder." Unfortunately, too many Evangelicals have hidden behind the "right to choose argument," the most dishonest of all positions.

Since the 1973 Supreme Court decision legalizing abortion, more than 8 million unborn babies have been killed by abortion. There is always at least one dead victim produced from this act of violence. Gary Bergel, in his pamphlet "Abortion in

America," outlines the five methods of abortion currently being practiced in America.

1. *D & C, or Dilatation and Curettage Abortion*—This method is most often used in the first thirteen weeks of pregnancy. A tiny, hoe-like instrument, the curette, is inserted into the womb through the dilated cervix, its natural gateway. The abortionist then scrapes the wall of the uterus, cutting the baby's body to pieces. This method is now used less frequently than suction.

2. *Suction Abortion*—This is the most commonly used method for early pregnancies; the principle is the same as in the D & C. In this technique, which was pioneered in Communist China, a powerful suction tube is inserted through the cervix into the womb. The body of the developing baby and placenta are torn to pieces and sucked into a jar.

3. *Salt Poisoning, or Hyper-Natremic Abortion*—This method is generally used after thirteen weeks of pregnancy. A long needle is inserted through the mother's abdomen, and a strong salt solution is injected directly into the amniotic fluid that surrounds the child. The salt is swallowed and "breathed" and slowly poisons the baby, burning his skin as well. The mother goes into labor about a day later and expels a dead, grotesque, shriveled baby. Some babies have survived the "salting out" and been born alive.

4. *Hysterotomy, or Caesarean Section Abortion*—This method is used in the last trimester of pregnancy. The womb is entered by surgery through the wall of the abdomen. The tiny baby is removed and allowed to die by neglect or is sometimes killed by a direct act.

5. *Prostaglandin Chemical Abortion*—This is the newest form of abortion. It uses chemicals developed and sold by the Upjohn Pharmaceutical Company of Kalamazoo, Michigan. These hormone-like compounds are injected or otherwise applied to the muscle of the uterus, causing it to contract intensely, thereby pushing out the developing baby. Babies have been decapitated during these abnormal contractions. Many have been born alive. The side effects to the mother are many. A number of mothers have even died from cardiac arrest when

the prostaglandin compounds were injected. Upjohn is one of the primary contemporary pharmaceutical firms known to have reverted to chemistry to cause death. Upjohn's 1979 annual report boldly declared that the company would promote these abortion chemicals in India and China during the coming decade.[2]

The abortion situation in our country didn't just explode upon us unexpectedly. A number of forces laid the foundation for this low view of life. Dr. Joseph Stanton of Boston has summarized this prelude:

> In the confluence of women's liberation, sexual freedom, and the concern for ecology, population and pollution, vast forces inimicable to the well-being of the human embryo and fetus were set in motion. The American Law Institute was proffering some reasonable liberalization of the abortion laws to take care of the so-called hard cases—physical and mental health, incest, rape and genetic defect. The "quality of human life" ethic gained respectability at the expense of human life itself in socially and academically impeccable circles. As medical indications for abortion evaporated, doctors increasingly invoked mental health as justification for abortion. Undocumented statements subsequently acknowledged as unfounded in truth were endlessly repeated until they acquired the ring of truth. Sincere and concerned people were disturbed. They were purposely and purposefully misled. Thousands of women were said to be dying each year at the hands of criminal abortionists. Some estimated 10,000 women died each year of criminal abortions; others said 5,000. Obviously, inflation hit the abortion statistics before it hit the grocery shelf.[3]

Though many unseen forces were working to prepare the way for our present abortion situation, the actual legal and social steps can be easily documented:

1967. The American Law Institute proposed a law that would allow abortion in cases of rape, incest, or a threat to the life or health of the mother, or in cases of grave defect in the child.

1969. The National Association for the Repeal of Abortion Laws formed and laid the groundwork for abortion on demand. Bernard Nathanson and Betty Friedan gave leadership.[4]

1970. On July 1, New York Gov. Nelson Rockefeller signed a law allowing licensed physicians in his state to perform abortions through the twenty-fourth week of pregnancy. New York City became an abortion capital.

1972. Janet Roe filed a suit to overturn a Texas law prohibiting her from having an abortion. The court ruled against her wish since her life was not in danger.

1973. The United States Supreme Court ruled the Texas court decision unconstitutional and, therefore, cancelled abortion laws in all fifty states. About this same time, *Doe* v. *Bolton* had other abortion-limiting provisions ruled unconstitutional. Thus every restriction against abortion on demand was removed.[5]

1973. One month after *Roe* v. *Wade,* the pro-abortion faction petitioned the federal courts to order city and state hospitals to make no charge to the poor and require that state and federal governments fund abortions for the poor as a part of Medicaid. The courts said yes.

1976. In September, U. S. Representative Henry Hyde sponsored the "Hyde Amendment," which restricts the federal funding of abortions to those necessary to save the life of the mother.

1979. The Supreme Court declared unconstitutional a Massachusetts law that required unmarried minor girls to get the approval of their parents before obtaining a legal abortion. Said the Court, "Every minor must have the opportunity—if she so desires—to go directly to a court without first consulting and notifying her parents."[6]

1980. U.S. District Judge John F. Dooling, Jr., of Brooklyn, New York, declared the "Hyde Amendment" unconstitutional. However, on June 30, the Supreme Court ruled by a vote of five to four that it was not unconstitutional.

These events have thrown the whole question of the sanctity of human life into focus. Paul K. Jewett, in an article entitled "The Relation of the Soul to the Fetus," has summarized the conflict:

> This marvelously endowed creature called man, whose intelligence reduces remote galaxies and minute atoms to the laws of

reason; who lives in the realm of responsibility, knowing the commendation of a good conscience and the condemnation of an evil one; who as Luther said, in his highest and noblest part is qualified to lay hold of the incomprehensible, invisible, and eternal, in short, to become the house where faith and God's Word are at home—is he or is he not a man while still in his mother's womb?[7]

Like most of the issues in this current study, the debate is not altogether a recent one. An Assyrian law dated between 1450 and 1250 B.C. prescribed death by torture in cases of procured abortion. Tertullian, the first theologian to speak on the subject, said that Christians abominate as murder both infanticide and abortion, the latter being a kind of murder in advance. For the embryonic man, according to Tertullian, was as the fruit to the blossom, destined in a little while to become a perfect man if nature met no disturbance.

Though only one Old Testament passage deals with the specific subject of abortion, there are several lines of biblical truth that should be considered before examining that pivotal passage.

First, the Bible asserts that *conception is a gift from God.* Eve, at the birth of Cain, declared that she had received him from the Lord (see Gen. 4:1). Sarah's belief that the Lord had restrained her from bearing (see Gen. 16:2) was confirmed when Abraham later received the divine assurance that she would have a son (see Gen. 17:19). Taking pity on Leah, the Lord "opened her womb" (Gen. 29:31), as He also did for Rachel (see Gen. 30:22). Of Ruth it is recorded that "the LORD gave her conception" (Ruth 4:13). Abortion scornfully discards a gift from the Almighty.

Second, the Bible teaches that *God is actively involved in fashioning the fetus:*

For thou hast possessed my reins: thou hast covered me in my mother's womb. I will praise thee; for I am fearfully and wonderfully made: marvelous are thy works; and that my soul knoweth right well. My substance was not hid from thee when I was made in secret, and curiously wrought in the lowest parts of the earth.[8] Thine eyes did see my substance, yet being unperfect; and in thy book all my members were written, which in continuance were fashioned, when as yet there was none of them (Ps. 139:13-16).

The purpose of this passage is basically to express a truth about God, but it also says something about the psalmist. It is obvious that David considered himself as having been a person even before he was conscious of himself. He was saying, "I, the person, was covered by Thy hand, O Lord, in my mother's womb. I was made in secret and curiously wrought in the inner recesses of my mother's body."

This same concept of the hand of God upon unborn life is suggested in other passages as well:

> Thine hands have made me and fashioned me together round about; yet thou dost destroy me. Remember, I beseech thee, that thou hast made me as the clay; and wilt thou bring me into dust again? . . . Thou hast clothed me with skin and flesh, and hast fenced me with bones and sinews. Thou hast granted me life and favor, and thy visitation hath preserved my spirit (Job 10:8-12).

> The burden of the word of the Lord for Israel, saith the Lord, which stretcheth forth the heavens, and layeth the foundation of the earth and formeth the spirit of man within him (Zech. 12:1).[9]

The abortionists seem to forget easily or perhaps refuse altogether to consider that from the very moment of conception, the hopes and dreams and plans of an almighty God are set in motion for each individual. G. A. D. Scott, a Canadian pastor, seemed to have this thought in mind when he wrote the following:

> Jesus said, "Let the little children come to me, and do not hinder them; for to such belongs the kingdom of God." You see, the destiny of every child conceived in the womb is the kingdom of God. In God's eyes children are not conceived to add to Canada's natural resources; they are not conceived for a life of bourgeois middle-aged selfishness; they are not conceived to play in bed and in cars hurtling to nowhere. The intention of God for every child conceived in the womb is that he grows up into God's kingdom, that he pass one day through the portals of death into life everlasting with God Himself. This is why Jesus said, "See that you do not despise one of these little ones."[10]

The pivotal Bible passage in this discussion is Exodus 21:22–25.

> If men strive, and hurt a woman with child, so that her fruit depart from her, and yet no mischief follows: he shall be surely punished, according as the woman's husband will lay upon him; and he shall pay as the judges determine. And if any mischief follow, then thou shalt give life for life, eye for eye, tooth for tooth, hand for hand, foot for foot, burning for burning, wound for wound, stripe for stripe.

Some have tried to make this text prove that God has a low regard for the unborn child compared to the newly born child. But a careful study of the passage yields the following interpretation: If a man in an argument with another man *accidentally* strikes a woman and she has a premature birth, there is to be a fine. Nothing here is premeditated. But if any further mischief is done—such as a deformity of the baby or the death of the baby as a result of the accident—the old law applies of an eye for an eye and a tooth for a tooth. Thus, this passage does not diminish the worth of an unborn child.

In the opinion of American law, however, unborn life is now very cheap. By September 1979 (just six-and-a-half years after the abortion decision), abortion at *whim* was urged as an ethical norm by ethicist John Fletcher. I am referring to the new ethical norm of aborting an unborn child because it is not the sex the parents want. [11]

While the pro-life Christian has built his case on the biblical position of the sanctity of life, the pro-abortionists have arrayed a whole arsenal of euphemistic arguments in support of abortion on demand. Some of the more popular are as follows:

1. *Every woman has the right to control her own body.* A woman has the right to decide whether she will bear a child. Of course, that is a true statement. The right is hers. But the decision should be made *before* conception. Said theologian Carl Henry:

> A Christian response to the abortion crisis encourages a new respect and sense of responsibility for the body and its use. A woman's body is not the domain and property of others. It is

hers to control, and she alone is responsible to God and to society for its use. When she yields that control, and through pregnancy is involved in intrapersonal relationships with a second party, and indeed to human society as a whole, it becomes too late for her to justify abortion on the basis of self-determination. The God of creation and redemption is also the guardian of the womb, however much abortion-on-demand would contradict or scorn such a conviction.[12]

The abortionists really don't practice their own dogma. While preaching that every woman has the right to control her own body, they deny unborn women that right by taking their lives before they are able to fight back.

2. *Abortion is necessary for special situations.* The argument for therapeutic abortion in special cases is another instance in which the situation ethicist uses the exception to determine the norm. The exceptions here are pregnancies resulting from rape or incest, or pregnancies that may endanger the life of the mother.

In order to evaluate this argument honestly, one must carefully consider the known facts.

Fact Number One—Abortions in this country for rape, incest, to protect the life of a mother, or to void a defective fetus make up less than 5 percent of all abortions. The rest are just for convenience, and we're talking about one million abortions per year.[13]

Fact Number Two—Rape almost never results in a pregnancy. Studies in Pennsylvania and Minnesota concerning rape and pregnancy show that as many as five thousand rapes have occurred successively without a single pregnancy.[14]

Fact Number Three—Protection of the life of the mother is a smokescreen. Dr. C. Everett Koop has practiced pediatric surgery for over thirty years. He has said that in his entire career, he has not known of a single instance in which the child had to be aborted to save the mother's life.[15]

3. *Every child should be a wanted child.* According to this argument, it is supposed to be kinder to the unborn child to abort it than to allow it to be born and possibly suffer mistreatment. Those who fought for liberalized abortion have had their

way. Since 1970, it is conservatively estimated in the United States that there are probably over 6 million fewer children than there would have been if abortion were still illegal. Since these 6 million were "unwanted" and supposedly would have been prime targets for child abuse, it would seem reasonable to look for a sharp drop in child abuse in this same period. But, in fact, since the legalization of abortion on demand, child abuse has grown remarkably, and it is not just due to more efficient reporting.[16]

In the *Roe* v. *Wade* and *Doe* v. *Bolton* decisions of 1973, the Supreme Court provided examples of factors that would guide women in concluding that a child was unwanted and, therefore, "abortable": If the child might "force upon the woman a distressful life or future"; if she might be "taxed by childcare"; if she would experience "embarrassment as a result of being unwed"; or if the birth of a child would "deprive a woman of her preferred lifestyle." With such criteria, surely our heavenly Father would have been justified in aborting all of us, for we are not the children He wanted! Surely we distress, tax, and embarrass Him. Surely we are not God's "children by choice," to use a pro-abortion slogan.[17]

According to a study prepared by Jan Gentles, a professor at York University in Toronto, Canada, based on a survey of five Canadian provinces,

> The fact that as abortion rises so, too, does abuse of born children is tragic proof that society's acquiescence in the expending of pre-born life tends to decline further the status of *older children*. This fact must force a rethinking of the issue. When Canadian figures are taken in conjunction with the American studies showing a positive correlation between wantedness and battering, the causal link becomes evident. Together the Canadian and U.S. experiences suggest that more abortion leads to more child abuse. This is not surprising since abortion *is* child abuse.[18]

Harold O. J. Brown rightly observes that parents could easily reason, "I didn't have to have him. I could have killed him before he was born. So, if I want to knock him around now that he is born, isn't that my right?"[19]

4. *Abortion is simply the termination of a pregnancy.* This is another attempt by the abortionists to defuse the emotional language of baby-killing. It allows us to deal with abortion in the abstract. It makes it possible for us to forget the fact that abortion does not take place upon the body of the woman, although she is obviously involved. Abortion does not take place upon a condition, although the condition—pregnancy—is altered as a result of it. The reality of abortion is that it kills an innocent human being. We may choose to call that baby such nonpersonal names as "uterine contents," "birth matter," and "the products of conception," but we cannot with our vague language depersonalize the object of God's creative love.[20]

5. *I believe abortion is wrong, but I think every person should have the right to choose.* This is a rather convenient way to be both for something and against it at the same time. Leave it to the politicians to come up with such a "diplomatic" solution. But it is not a solution. We don't reason that way in other realms. Would you vote for a president or a congressman who openly stated that though he was personally opposed to murder, he would grant to each individual the right to choose? Try such logic on the crimes of rape, theft, assault and battery, and so on.

In her book *Who Broke the Baby?*, Mrs. Garten includes this parody on the Good Samaritan story:

A certain man went down from Jerusalem to Jericho and fell among thieves, who stripped him of his raiment, and wounded him, and departed, leaving him half dead.

And by chance there came down a certain priest that way and when he saw him, perhaps he thought, "Well, I wouldn't rob a traveler myself, but I support the right of others to choose," for he passed by on the other side.

And likewise, a Levite, when he was at that place, came and looked on him, but, perhaps, he thought, "Every man should be a wanted man, and obviously this one wasn't," for he too passed by on the other side.

But, a certain Samaritan, as he journeyed came where he was; and when he saw him, he had compassion on him and history has forever called him good.[21]

The abortion battle is one that every Christian should be willing to fight. We must become knowledgeable about the problem. We must learn the strategy of the enemy and become adept at seeing through the vague and euphemistic arguments they use. We should consider joining a pro-life group. For too long, Protestant Evangelicals have stood on the sidelines while the Roman Catholics carried the banner in this conflict. We should make sure we know where our political candidates stand on these issues and vote in accordance with our biblical convictions regardless of party affiliation. We should do all within our power to push through an amendment to our Constitution guaranteeing the right to life of every unborn child. We should develop a deep compassion for the woman whose circumstances might cause her to consider abortion, ministering to her in every way possible.

If we do not do at least these things, we can expect that within the next decade the following will occur:

- Infanticide, now practiced illegally behind closed doors, will become legal and eventually, for certain types of deformity, may be mandatory.
- Through the "living will," passive euthanasia will become so much a part of our culture that active euthanasia will be adopted.
- It may become illegal for an obstetrician to deliver a baby with a congenital defect if that defect could have been detected before birth and the baby aborted.
- In ten years, it may be difficult for a Christian physician to practice medicine in this country as a matter of conscience.
- America may become another 1930 Germany through the wedding of corrupt law and corrupt medicine. Many of the legal and medical attitudes that were dominant in Germany in the 1930s are in our society today.[22]

As the blood of Abel cried out to God from the ground, the cries of unborn babies call out to us from the womb. Listen carefully and with compassion:

May 5—Today my life began! My parents do not know yet. I am as small as a seed of an apple! A little "sprout!" Probably my sex and color of eyes are settled!

May 19 (day 14). Some think I'm not a real person yet. I am not a loaf of bread. But I am a weak crumb!

May 23 (day 18). My mouth is just beginning to open now! Just think! In a year or so, I shall be laughing and later talking! I know what my first word will be: "Mama!"

May 25 (day 20). My heart began to beat today all by itself! From now on, it shall gently beat for the rest of my life without ever stopping to rest!

June 2 (day 28). I am growing a bit every day! My arms and legs are beginning to take shape! Some day I shall climb up and hug my mama and daddy!

June 12 (day 38). Tiny fingers are beginning to form on my hands. Funny how small they are! I'll be able to stroke my mother's hair with them!

June 20 (day 46). Today the doctor told Mom that I am living under her heart. O how happy she must be! Are you happy, Mom?

June 25 (day 51). Mom and Dad are probably thinking about a name for me. I am getting so big already!

July 10 (day 66). My hair is growing! It is smooth and bright and shiny! Wonder what kind of hair Mom has.

July 13 (day 69). I am just about able to see! It is dark around me. When Mom brings me into the world, it will be full of sunshine and flowers! But what I want more than anything is to see my mother!

July 24 (day 80). I wonder if Mom hears the whispering of my heart? Some children are born a little sick. But my heart is strong and healthy! It beats so evenly! "Tup-tup, Tup-tup." You'll have a healthy baby, Mommy!

July 28 (day 84). Today my mother killed me.

NOTES

1. Charles C. Ryrie, *You Mean the Bible Teaches That* (Chicago: Moody, 1974), p. 86.
2. Gary Bergel, *Abortion in America* (Elyria, OH: Intercessors for America, 1980), p. 4.
3. J. R. Stanton, *Abortion: Flawed Premise and Promise*, NSA delivered many occasions.

4. Bernard Nathanson later repudiated his pro-abortion stand and wrote *Aborting America,* one of the strongest indictments of abortion on demand currently in print.

5. Justice Blackmun wrote the majority opinion of the Supreme Court decision. He said that once the fetus was viable—that is, able to exist on its own outside the womb—the state could regulate or even prohibit abortion. The Pennsylvania legislature passed a law requiring that if the victim of an intended abortion might be viable, the doctor must use the abortion technique "which would provide the best opportunity for the fetus to be aborted alive." This law was struck down, however, by the Supreme Court in January 1979. It was Justice Blackmun who said that Pennsylvania had taken that initiative too far.

6. Justice Byron White had this to say about the Supreme Court's Massachusetts decision: "The court now holds it unconstitutional for a state to require that in all cases parents receive notice that their daughter seeks an abortion, and if they object to abortion, an opportunity to participate in a hearing that will determine it is in the best interest of the child to undergo surgery."

7. Paul K. Jewett, "The Relation of the Soul to the Fetus," *Christianity Today,* November 8, 1968, p. 7.

8. The phrase "lowest parts of the earth" is a Hebrew expression to describe the dark interior of the womb.

9. Other passages that speak of prenatal consciousness are Genesis 25:22, 23; Ecclesiastes 11:5; Jeremiah 1:5; Luke 1:41, 44; and Galatians 1:15-16.

10. G. A. D. Scott, *Abortion, the Last Resort* (1968 United Church of Canada-Renewal Fellowship).

11. C. Everett Koop, "Abortion and Euthanasia," in *Turning Point,* comp. Roger Elwood (Cincinnati: Standard Publishing, 1980), p. 46.

12. Carl F. H. Henry, "Abortion," *Christian Heritage* 32 (February 1971), p. 25. Published by Christ's Mission, Hackensack, N.J.

13. C. Everett Koop, "Deception on Demand," *Moody Monthly,* May 1980, p. 28.

14. Ibid.

15. Ibid., p. 25.

16. Francis A. Schaeffer and C. Everett Koop, *Whatever Happened to the Human Race?* (Old Tappan, NJ: Revell, 1979), pp. 35, 36.

17. Jean Staker Garten, *Who Broke the Baby?* (Minneapolis: Bethany Fellowship, 1979), p. 33.

18. *International Life Times,* December 28, 1979.

19. Francis A. Schaeffer and C. Everett Koop, *Whatever Happened to the Human Race?,* p. 36.

20. Jean Staker Garten, *Who Broke the Baby?,* p. 36.

21. Ibid. pp. 99, 100.

22. C. Everett Koop, "Abortion and Euthanasia," p. 49.

CHAPTER
FOUR

Secret Thoughts

I hold it true that thoughts are things
Endowed with bodies, breath, and wings,
And that we send them forth to fill
The world with good results . . . or ill.

That which we call our secret thought,
Speeds to the earth's remotest spot,
And leaves its blessings or its woes
Like tracks behind it as it goes.

It is God's law. Remember it
In your still chamber as you sit
With thoughts you would not dare have known,
And yet make comrades when alone.

These thoughts have life; and they will fly
And leave their impress by and by,
Like some marsh breeze, whose poisoned
   breath
Breathes into homes its fevered breath.

And after you have quite forgot
Or all outgrown some vanished thought,
Back to your mind to make its home,
A dove or raven, it will come.

Then let your secret thoughts be fair;
They have a vital part and share
In shaping worlds and molding fate . . .
God's system is so intricate.

Ella Wilcox Wheeler

IS PORNOGRAPHY ADULT ENTERTAINMENT?

MARTY WAS A seventeen-year-old son of an affluent family who was sent to a psychiatrist because of recurrent, unexplained headaches. Headaches weren't his real problem, though. His real problem began four years earlier when Marty was in junior high school. He was bright and he was popular, having no difficulties in school whatsoever. One afternoon, a friend of Marty's invited him and some other girls and boys of about the same age of twelve or thirteen to come over to his house and watch a movie that his parents showed at grown-up parties. The movie turned out to be a hard-core pornographic film, depicting sexual perversion of the worst kind. After the initial embarrassment, the kids were completely seduced. They began to try to outdo the adults from that moment on. By the time Marty had reached high school, he no longer engaged in any promiscuity; he stopped because he no longer got a kick out of it. He turned now to drugs and sexual fantasies. Marty's experiences with pornography sated him with sex before the process of idealization was established in his relationships with girls. Apart from a miracle, Marty will never lead a normal life.[1]

What happened to Marty could happen to your children or to mine, because pornography is on the rampage in almost every segment of society. Each year, the industry that produces "adult" products of one kind or another chalks up at least $4 billion in profit. That is as much as the legitimate movie and record industries make combined. Six of the most profitable newsstand monthlies are now "male entertainment" magazines. Over 500,000 children are used as models in the "child porn" industry. A recent publication on syndicated child pornography noted that over 280 monthly publications are produced in America on that subject alone.

Pornography is one of the most unselective evil influences in our society. Gambling is restricted to adults. Tobacco is not to be sold to anyone under eighteen. Alcohol is not to be sold to minors. But every time your children and mine walk past the average drugstore magazine rack, the ugly demon of pornography stares out at them. Though most stores have tried to camouflage the blatant sex magazines by covering the racks, the pruriently written smut is still accessible through the paperback book racks in the back of the store.

The word *pornography* is derived from two words, *porno*, meaning "prostitute," and *graphei* meaning "writing." Thus, the word means the writing of prostitutes or writing about prostitutes. Webster's dictionary defines it as "the depiction of erotic behavior (as in pictures or writing) intended to cause sexual excitement." A modern-day definition includes this in its meaning: "arousing sexual drives of deviations, perversions, and abnormal behavior." In the words of the Longford Report of 1972, "Pornography is that which exploits and dehumanizes sex, so that human beings are treated as things and women, in particular, as sex objects."

The aggressive, open marketing of pornographic sex began in 1955. Hugh Hefner, with little money and a center-page foldout of a nude Marilyn Monroe, bargained the *Playboy* theme into a $170 million empire—one of the most amazing financial success stories in journalistic history. *Playboy*'s circulation has been put at 5,900,000 per month. Newsstand sales bring the figure to 11,000,000, and each magazine is said to be read by seven people. According to its own advertisements, *Playboy* is read by three out of four males in college and one out of every two men under thirty-five in professional and managerial occupations.

Hefner's magazine has led the way in communicating pornography through pictures and carefully planned and written articles attacking Judeo-Christian morality. On one occasion, he wrote these words: "If Christ were here today, and had to choose between being on the staff of *Playboy Magazine* or being on the staff of one of the joy-killing, pleasure-denying churches, he would, of course, immediately join us."

During the twenty years following the birth of *Playboy*, one hundred competitors followed, crowding good magazines off the newsstands. No one ever dreamed that the competition in filth would eventually excrete a magazine like *Hustler*, sold everywhere and currently boasting a serious challenge to *Playboy's* circulation records.

In 1957, the industry was helped when the United States Supreme Court ruled that material wasn't illegal just because it contained explicit sexual scenes. To be obscene, it had to treat sex "in a manner appealing to prurient (lewd) interests" and be "utterly without redeeming social importance." In 1973, the Court took what was considered a more conservative stand. It ruled that a local jury should decide what is obscene, according to the community's standards.

But the plague is not limited to the printed page alone. Can anyone deny that movies are dirtier than ever? They do not call it dirt. They call it "realism." The movie industry's announcement that perversion and homosexuality would no longer be barred from the screen, provided the subjects were handled with "delicacy and taste," opened the door for an even lower level of decency in the industry. And that which has not been barred from the screen is now no longer barred from the home either. Double and triple X-rated movies are now available through cable TV. They are being sold in stores on video cassettes and little by little are creeping into our prime time television. Children left unattended for a short time in many homes could be exposed to the rawest of pornography just by turning the TV dial in the wrong direction.

And pornography has found another way to market its smut. A recent article in a leading news magazine, on the show business and TV page, describes what is called "Orgasmic Rock." The performers of this music seem to be proud in saying, "This is music to commit adultery with." Disc-hungry teenagers are buying the filthy records, and radio stations are playing them on the air.

Recently a troubled mother wrote the following letter to Ann Landers:

Dear Ann Landers: Most parents have no idea what rock music is all about because they pay no attention to it. If they listened to the lyrics they'd be shocked. For example, "Get Down and Make Love" tells a story of homosexual love. Another, "Cold Ethyl" by Alice Cooper, is an incredibly vulgar song celebrating sexual perversion. "Wild Love" by Frank Zappa is a thoroughly offensive number. The words to "Some Girls" (Rolling Stones) could not be printed in a family newspaper. Acceptance of marital infidelity is the theme of many rock songs, such as "Part-Time Love."

Ann replied: I've been hearing about the filthy rock and roll lyrics for a long time and decided to tune in and listen. Twenty-three years of this column have made me virtually shockproof, but some of the lyrics were incredibly crude and offensive.[2]

We are drowning our young people in violence, cynicism, and sadism. Someone has observed that the grandchildren of the kids who used to weep because the little match girl froze to death now feel cheated if she is not slugged, raped, and thrown into a furnace.

One clear principle of the Word of God is this: The seeds of destruction are contained in every sin. James 1:15 puts it this way: "Then when lust hath conceived, it bringeth forth sin: and sin, when it is finished, bringeth forth death." Galatians 6:7, 8 says, "Be not deceived; God is not mocked: for whatever a man soweth, that shall he also reap. For he that soweth to his flesh shall of the flesh reap corruption."

Someday, if she does not return to righteousness, America will reap what she has sown. Therefore, Christians must not let go unchallenged the flood of pornography that involves the exploitation of the weaknesses of man and the corruption of his spiritual and moral nature. Pornography makes a woman an object of lust rather than a person made in the image of God. Pornography, in attacking the image of God in man, is an attack upon God Himself, and God will not be mocked.

PORNOGRAPHY IS HAVING A DESTRUCTIVE EFFECT UPON OUR CULTURE.

One definition of culture is this: "The integrated pattern of human behavior that includes thought, speech, and action."

God through revelation has given to us the boundaries that define our culture. The moral laws that originated with God are the safeguards that are built into our behavioral patterns. When we disregard those laws, we destroy the pattern, and the process of death sets in. That which we know as crime is the disregard for those laws. There is no one influence in our society that is contributing to sexual crime more than pornography. Years ago, J. Edgar Hoover, writing in *This Week Magazine*, bewailed pornography's influence on crime in our country:

> What we do know is that an overwhelmingly large number of cases of sex crime is associated with pornography. We know that sex criminals read it and are clearly influenced by it. . . . I believe pornography is a major source of sex violence. I believe that if we eliminate the distribution of such items, we shall greatly reduce our crime rate.[3]

Hoover's comments are supported by the facts. Press and police investigators noted the quantities of pornography in David Berkowitz's (New York City's "Son of Sam" killer) apartment and in Charles Manson's commune. Dr. Natalie Shainess of New York and Dr. Frank Osanka of Illinois report a growing resistance to therapy among convicted rapists who no longer view their acts as socially aberrant.[4]

Pornography consists no longer of seedy entrepreneurs slobbering along society's lunatic fringe. It is a major industry tied in with organized crime, prostitution, sex-slave kidnapping rings, and drug peddling. Ralph Salerno, a retired New York City detective who is an expert on organized crime, has been quoted as seeing a trend toward the open involvement of mobsters in the "sex business." He explains that their willingness to make a profit from pornography is linked to the fact that it no longer has a bad image. It's both profitable and acceptable.[5]

Police vice squads report that 77 percent of the child molesters of boys and 87 percent of the child molesters of girls admitted trying out, or imitating, the sexual behavior modeled by pornography. In one group of rapists, 57 percent indicated they had tried out the sexual behavior they had seen depicted in pornography. The Michigan state police, in a recent study of

35,000 sex crimes over a twenty-year period, found that 43 percent were pornography related. These are the cases in which the perpetrator was apprehended. No one knows how many crimes have been inspired by pornography in cases where the perpetrator has never been caught.[6]

Accompanying the flood of pornography, we have seen a huge increase in venereal disease. We even have an epidemic of gonorrhea of the throat. Doctors are being advised to do cultures for gonorrhea in all persistent sore throats.[7]

A recent fad in the porn industry is what they call "snuff" films or "slasher" films. These productions show the actual murder and dismemberment of an unsuspecting actress on the screen. There have been several of these films circulating our land at the same time.[8] Proverbs 27:20 says, "Hell and destruction are never full; so the eyes of man are never satisfied." A man who sets out on a journey of self-indulgence will ultimately die at the hand of his own lust.

A casual glance at the lists of the sins of the flesh recorded in the New Testament will reveal that the sins of sexual looseness are grouped together with the sins of violence. They always go hand in hand. We should not be surprised to see it today (see Rom. 1:26-31; Gal. 5:19-21; Eph. 5:3,11).

Lord Devlin, the famous British jurist, in a book entitled *The Enforcement of Morals,* wrote, "A sense of right and wrong is necessary for the life of a community. Without it the society will destroy itself. History shows that the loosening of moral bonds is the first stage of disintegration."[9] J. D. Unwin, a British social anthropologist, spent several years studying the birth and death of civilizations. In *Sex and Culture,* Unwin reported:

> The energy which holds society together is sexual in nature. When a man is devoted to one woman and one family, he is motivated to build, save, protect, plan and prosper on their behalf. However, when his sexual interests are dispersed, and generalized, his effort is invested in the gratification of sensual desires. Any human society is free to display great energy or to enjoy sexual freedom. They cannot do both for more than one generation. History reveals that entire societies deteriorate when free love reaches a position of social acceptance.[10]

Pornography constitutes a direct attack on significant relationships because it helps create a mind-set that eventually treats all people as sexual objects. Modern pornography is an education system. It teaches. Its message is: Human beings are mere animals; the highest value is immediate pleasure; other people may be used and abused and then discarded. It teaches that sex is divorced from love, commitment, morality, and responsibility, that perversion is to be preferred to normality, that women are fair game for anyone who cares to exploit them. John H. Court, in his book *Pornography: A Christian Critique,* addresses the philosophical implications of pornography:

> And it is precisely on the level of meaning, not merely on the level of personal issues, that pornography challenges the Biblical and human perspective. For pornography is significant not simply because of the existence of a whole industry of exploitation, but because it represents a philosophy of man which is fundamentally not only anti-Christian but also anti-human. It raises questions about the dignity of men and women, the limits of human freedom, the purpose of sexuality, and the welfare of children, as well as the moral status of sexual deviations. Therefore, from the perspective of man as created in God's image, an essential characteristic of pornography is its evil abuse not only of sexuality, but of human nature itself. The pervasiveness of such an evil is something not to be ignored but confronted.[11]

Psychoanalyst Ernest van den Haag says pornography actually could cause the breakdown of society: "Pornography invites us to perceive others only as pieces of meat, as exploitation for the sake of our own sensations." Van den Haag thinks obscene material might thus destroy the social bonds that are formed by our caring enough to make sacrifices for each other.[12]

Harold Janz, writing in *Christian Heritage Magazine,* reported that when he visited the Soviet Union, he was amazed at the outward puritanism of that society. The constant bombardment with sexual messages that we've become used to here simply does not exist there. Almost every communist state has virtually wiped out the trade in pornographic magazines, books, and films—not because the majority of people desire it, but because someone or some small leadership group feels it is in the best interest of the society to remove it.[13] We know that their reasons are not godly or biblical. Could it be that they recognize the threat of pornography to their society?

WHY DON'T WE DO SOMETHING?

A national opinion research study in 1978 found that 57 percent of Americans are convinced that pornography leads to a breakdown of morals and encourages the crime of rape. Yet, the pornography industry continues to grow each year. Why is it so difficult to combat its proliferation?

In a recent *Christianity Today* editorial, the following six reasons were given:

1. Police are unable to find the producers of pornography and end up making inconsequential arrests of the peddlers instead.
2. The Supreme Court's vague definition of obscenity makes it difficult for local governments to apply it.
3. Most people are ignorant of the exact nature and pervasiveness of smut.
4. Many who realize the seriousness of the problem are unwilling to take the trouble to get involved.
5. Some Americans soothe their consciences by labeling their moral indifference as tolerance.
6. The first amendment, which guarantees freedom of speech, is perverted to the benefit of pornographers.[14]

But there are some things that concerned Christians can do to keep this disease from spreading any further. We can examine our cities' zoning ordinances, which might help restrict street advertising and newsstand displays. We can exercise our consumer rights by not supporting publishers and producers who traffic in pornography. We can refuse to buy products produced by firms that sponsor smut shows on TV.

We can urge newspapers to restrict pornographic advertising, as the *New York Times* and a few other papers have done. We can speak out in disgust against those who claim to have been born again, yet continue to produce filth that belongs in the gutter.

Most of all, we can make sure that we keep *ourselves* unspotted by the world. With the constant bombardment facing Christians every day, more than a few have succumbed to the temptation. Recently, I learned of a gospel minister who attended late-night pornographic films until he was discovered by one of his parishioners who had also fallen into the sin of an unclean mind.

Keeping ourselves pure before God will not come easy to modern Christians. Without a plan to deal with this area of life, all of us are subject to defeat. Perhaps the following suggestions will help those who struggle in this matter:

1. *Covenant with your eyes.* Job did (see Job 31:1), and it's a good suggestion for all of us. The eyes provide the window to the mind. Most problems, especially for men, start here. By the power of the Holy Spirit, we can be disciplined in the use of our eyes.

2. *Consecrate your mind.* When Paul urged the Romans to present their bodies as sacrifices to the Lord, he included a special reference to the mind: "Be ye transformed by the renewing of your mind" (Rom. 12:2). The Bible warns us to keep our hearts pure, for out of it are the issues of life. Our thinking ultimately determines our character. Solomon said, "As a man thinketh in his heart, so is he" (Prov. 28:7). Jesus explained to His disciples that the heart was the seat of indwelling sins: "For from within, out of the heart of men, proceed evil thoughts, adulteries, fornications, murders, thefts, covetousness, wickedness, deceit, lasciviousness, an evil eye, blasphemy, pride, foolishness: All these evil things come from within, and defile the man" (Mark 7:21-23).

On another occasion, He taught them, "The good man out of the good treasure of his heart brings forth what is good; and the evil man out of the evil treasure brings forth what is evil; for the mouth speaks from that which fills his heart" (Luke 6:45 NASB).

The mind is the battleground upon which every moral and spiritual battle is fought. As far back as Noah, this has been true. When God saw the "great wickedness" of Noah's day, He perceived that every intent of the thoughts of man's heart "was only evil continually" (Gen. 6:5).

3. *Commit yourself to Bible memorization.* Paul taught the Philippians that prayer would cause the peace of God to guard their minds. But he did not hesitate to command them to "think on," or let their minds dwell on, things that were honest, just, pure, lovely, and of good report (see Phil. 4:6-8).

Christians are responsible for "bringing into captivity every thought to the obedience of Christ" (2 Cor. 10:5). There is only one way to accomplish this goal: We must fill our minds with God's Word. The psalmist had this in mind when he wrote, "Wherewithal shall a young man cleanse his way? by taking heed thereto according to thy word. . . . Thy word have I hid in mine heart, that I might not sin against thee" (Ps. 119:9, 11). When we have committed many passages of God's Word to memory, we will discover that they come to our minds, at just the right moment, to aid us in gaining victory in this battle.

4. *Counteract Satan's strategy in your life.* Paul told the Corinthians that he was not ignorant of Satan's devices (see 2 Cor. 2:11). We should follow his example. I am convinced that as Satan goes about seeking whom he may devour, he has a definite strategy for each of us. I am quite often surprised by the consistency of sinning Christians. Same time, same place, same companions, same circumstances, over and over again. Satan knows our weaknesses and uses all the tools at his command to keep us constantly in great spiritual jeopardy. When will we learn that there are certain places and situations that promote sin in our lives? It may be the magazine rack in the airport newsstand, the local theater, the movie channel on your TV set, the "adult" bookstore you have to pass on your way to work. Whatever it is, we must determine not to give our enemy an advantage. Stay away from the airport magazine racks, don't go to the theater, discontinue cable TV, take another route home. Don't knowingly put yourself in the place of defeat. Certainly Paul had this in mind when he wrote these words to the Romans: "Neither yield ye your members as instruments of unrighteousness unto sin but yield yourselves unto God, as those that are alive from the dead, and your

members as instruments of righteousness unto God" (Rom. 6:13).

Some time ago, after preaching a message on the subject of pornography on our television program, I received this letter from a man who had watched the service many hundreds of miles away:

Dear Pastor Jeremiah,

I was sitting here in my room contemplating going out and having a beer and possibly looking upon porno flicks or whatever else the night might bring. As I was getting ready to go out, I turned on the TV and your program was being shown. I listened with great interest as you uncovered my life story. It seems almost as if you received your sermon from the files in my head.

Down deep as I search myself, I know I am doing wrong. I, at times, feel guilty about the things I do. I cannot honestly say that I enjoy getting drunk, nor do I enjoy subjecting myself to the filth that is associated with the sex market. From time to time, I find myself getting up in the middle of a triple X movie out of sheer disgust over what I see on the screen.

I am a happily married man, and I have three beautiful children. I know my wife would flip if she knew what I do when I am away from home. . . . I feel so dirty now, and I hope somehow you can make sense out of what I've said. I have turned my back on God and sometimes I feel as though He has given up on me.

You spoke of being saved. How do you really know? Tonight I sit here with tears in my eyes, and I don't know why. Please help me if you can!

The message of hope for this man is the message of hope for each and every man whose life is weighted down by the sin of evil thoughts. "Come now, and let us reason together, saith the Lord: though your sins be as scarlet, they shall be as white as snow; though they be red like crimson, they shall be as wool" (Isa. 1:18). "The blood of Jesus Christ . . . cleanseth from all sin" (1 John 1:7). That promise applies to the sin of the unclean mind.

Paul reminded the Corinthians that even though some of them had been fornicators, idolaters, adulterers, effeminate, abusers of themselves with mankind, thieves, covetous, drunkards, revilers, and extortioners, yet nonetheless, they had been washed clean "in the name of the Lord Jesus" (1 Cor. 6:11).

Edmund Burke never spoke more eloquently than when he spoke of his beloved Britain:

> Men are qualified for civil liberty in exact proportion to their disposition to moral chains upon their own appetites. . . .
> Society cannot exist unless a controlling power upon will and appetite be placed somewhere; and the less of it there is within, the more there must be without. It is ordained in the eternal constitution of things that men of intemperate minds cannot be free.

For the true Christian, Jesus Christ and the indwelling Spirit provide the "inward control." But there is no evidence to suggest that enough Spirit-filled Christians live in our society to do away with the need for the "power without" that God's laws and good government provide us.

In E. M. Blaiklock's commentary on Romans 1:26-32, he speaks to Christians' responsibility in a sexually permissive society:

> The close of this chapter is a warning to all peoples and all ages. To read it in our own "permissive society" is to encounter a challenge to be strong in faith, determined in our committal to God, urgent in our evangelism. Paul is describing a society which had abandoned God. He is diagnosing the malady from which Rome was to die, for no great nation has ever been destroyed by a foe from without which has not already destroyed itself by corruption within. Such sin carries its own penalty, its own damnation. The time is here when Christians must show, as they were called upon to do in Rome, by word, act and manner of life, their difference.[15]

NOTES

1. *Moral Majority Report*, July 1, 1980, p. 2.
2. Reprint permission granted by Field Newspaper Syndicate, Chicago, IL.

3. Neil Gallagher, *How To Stop the Porno Plague* (Minneapolis: Bethany, 1977), p. 19.
4. Robin Morgan, "How to Run the Pornographers Out of Town and Preserve the First Amendment," *Ms. Magazine*, November 1978, p. 55.
5. Ibid.
6. *Washington Weekly*, June 10, 1980.
7. Ibid.
8. Neil Gallagher, *How To Stop the Porno Plague*, p. 14.
9. Lord Devlin, *The Enforcement of Morals*, quoted by Harold Janz, "Facing the Pornography Issue," *Christian Heritage*, March 1976, p. 7.
10. J. D. Unwin, *Sex and Culture* (London: Oxford University, 1934), p. 414.
11. John H. Court, *Pornography: A Christian Critique* (Downers Grove, IL: InterVarsity, 1980), p. 9.
12. Elizabeth Sendor, "Why Can't We Stamp Out Pornography," *Senior Scholastic*, n.d., p. 18.
13. Harold Janz, "Facing the Pornography Issue," p. 5.
14. *Christianity Today*, June 27, 1980, p. 10.
15. E. M. Blaiklock, *Daily Bible Commentary* (London: Scripture Union, 1973), pp. 27, 28.

CHAPTER
FIVE

In God We Trust

In God, we trust, O nation highly favoured,
We trust in God to save us from our foes;
Our Victor He, almighty to deliver,
What need we more? our ev'ry need He
    knows.

In God we trust, let others trust their rulers;
We trust in God to save us from alarm;
Like broken reeds, the works of man will fail
    us,
Our God alone can keep us from all harm.

In God we trust, O people of His choosing,
We trust in God to save us from our greed,
That we unselfishly may live for others,
And to His Word may hearken and take heed.

In God we trust, O land of Heaven's blessing,
We trust in God to save us from our sin;
Our fleshly walk, our laws and standards,
    broken,
Proclaim our need of righteousness within.

Oswald J. Smith

IS THE NEW MORALITY MORAL?

NEVER BEFORE HAVE the headlines of America's newspapers told such a sordid story. Bribery, arson, kickbacks, moral corruption in high places, "Watergate," and countless other forms of dishonesty tell the story of a nation whose moral code has gone wild. It is even worse that we have accepted the fact that, given a chance, all too many Americans—whether they are high school students, government officials, film magnates, purchasing agents, or whoever—will cheat.

We accept lies from the repairman and the chairman of the board, all as a matter of course, and as an institutional habit of the times. We accept lies from the government; and the dishonesty of politicians is, at present, so pervasive that it has ceased to be a comedian's joke.

Campus surveys show that one-third of our college students say they would cheat if they were sure they would not be caught. Forty-five percent say they do not think it is necessary to lead a moral life in order to be happy or successful.

Honorable members of the bar are today appalled at the increase in the number of shysters in the practice of law. A recent congressional investigation of medical practices turned up the horrifying fact that American doctors, greedy for Medicare fees, are annually performing thousands of unnecessary operations, inflicting unnecessary pain on helpless and trusting patients for profit.[1]

Ivan Hill, writing in *Leadership Magazine,* explains that our conduct is not the result of ignorance: "More than 86% of all people interviewed associated ethics with standards and rules of conduct, morals, and right and wrong, values and honesty.

77

People immediately understand that although ethics may not appear in the headlines, the story told is about the lack of ethics—the doing of wrong as opposed to right."[2]

Robert Ringer is one of the great champs of this current trend. He writes books in which he, himself, is the main figure. His first title was *Winning Through Intimidation*—in other words, how to be a wolf, or a cat, or a fox and gain personal advantage through preying on others. Then he wrote *Looking Out for Number One*. By number one, he means "me, myself." He wrote the book "to make as much money as possible." It is a new rendition of the very old sin of selfishness. The book topped the best-seller lists for non-fiction for a whole year. The remarkable thing is that Robert Ringer turns selfishness—plain old "I love me"—into a nobility. He presents it as a dramatic rebirth of amorality: "Clear your mind, then . . . forget the moral standards others may have tried to cram down your throat."[3]

WHERE DID IT START?

When we contemplate a generation that has forgotten the difference between right and wrong, we cannot help but wonder where it all started. Though this amoral philosophy is often described as "The New Morality," it is in essence very old. As far back as 400 B.C., Epicurus championed these same ideas under the guise of Hedonism. He found deep pleasure in philosophical meditation, but he managed to produce disciples who became known for finding deeper meaning and pleasure in sensual self-gratification.

In some measure, then, it is correct to say that this amoral philosophy has always been with us. The term "New Morality," however, came recently from an Anglican bishop, John A. T. Robinson. In 1963, he published a book entitled *Honest to God*. This book was a reexamination of Christian belief and contained a chapter with the title "The New Morality," which outlines this philosophy. Later on in 1963, Robinson delivered three lectures on "Christian Morals Today" at the Liverpool Cathedral. In his lectures, he argued that the old morality perverted the New Testament by teaching slavery to a legalistic code rather than absolute loyalty to the demands of Christ-like love.

In 1966, Joseph Fletcher joined the team of the New Moralists. This former dean of St. Paul's Cathedral in Cincinnati, Ohio, had recently become a professor of social ethics at the Episcopal Theological School in Cambridge, Massachusetts, and was a well-known author in both the United States and England. His support of the New Morality was documented in two volumes: *Situation Ethics: The New Morality* and *Moral Responsibility,* published in 1966 and 1967.

One other man should be mentioned among the advocates of the New Morality. Hugh Hefner is the son of devout Methodists who taught him a rigid and puritanical moral code. He rebelled against his parents' views and, in 1953, started *Playboy Magazine* with six hundred dollars of his own money, six thousand dollars of borrowed money, and a nude picture of Marilyn Monroe. He parlayed his ideas into a $70 million empire.

Perhaps no other publication of the twentieth century has so popularized the New Morality. *Playboy* is far more than "a girlie magazine." It contains more than party jokes, photographs of nude women, and cartoons that make fun of fornication and adultery. It promotes the view that man's sole goal should be the pursuit of pleasure and self-fulfillment, and it communicates this view cleverly and with great sophistication. It is dressed in the latest styles and equipped with gourmet food, fast sports cars, and palatial bachelor quarters.

WHAT IS THE NEW MORALITY?

The New Morality is a revolt against the principles and guidelines of God's Word. It is a permissiveness that says, "If no one is hurt, anything goes." It is built upon a humanistic philosophy that believes man is basically good and, given the right education, job, and environment, will make the right and loving choices.

According to Fletcher, all laws, codes, and rules are outmoded, obsolete, and no longer binding on mankind. The only authoritative law is the law of love: "Anything and everything is right or wrong according to the situation,"[4] and "the goal is to find absolute love's relative course."[5]

Some of his maxims: "The commandment [love] is a normative ideal, it is not an operational directive. All else, all other generalities [e.g., 'one should tell the truth' and 'one should respect life'] are at most only maxims, never rules. For the situationist, there are no rules—none at all."[6] "If people do not believe it is wrong to have sex outside of marriage, it isn't, unless they hurt themselves, their partners, or others."[7] "The New Morality, situation ethics, declares that everything is right or wrong according to the situation. And this candid approach is indeed a revolution in morals."[8]

In presenting his case, Fletcher advances six propositions that in themselves summarize the theory of the New Morality: (1) Love only is always good; (2) Love is the only norm; (3) Love and justice are the same; (4) Love is not liking; (5) Love justifies its means; and (6) Love decides there and then. Unfortunately, these propositions cannot be elaborated here, but they are plainly six aspects of the same basic premise: "When we say that love is always good, what we mean is that whatever is loving in any particular situation is good."[9]

So situation ethics, or the New Morality, recognizes a solitary absolute, the absolute of love, and it regards all other laws as relative to this one unbreakable imperative. All other laws may be broken, if necessary, in order that the law of love remain unbroken.

As an illustration, Fletcher tells the story of the rainmaker from the play by M. Richard Nash. The rainmaker made his living by convincing ranchers that he could bring rain for their parched crops. While at a particular ranch, the rainmaker feels sorry for the rancher's daughter who is a lonely, spinsterish individual. In order to restore this poor girl's sense of womanliness, he commits fornication with her. The girl's brother finds out the next morning and threatens to shoot the rainmaker. However, his wise, old rancher-father grabs the gun from his son and says, "Noah, you're so full of what's right you can't see what's good."

There you have in Fletcher's own illustration the concept of situationalism and the New Morality. According to this story, love is to be understood in terms of good intentions and desirable consequences. In other words, the end justifies the means. But sometimes good intentions and desirable consequences are in conflict with each other.

Take, for example, the Old Testament character Joseph. When he refused the immoral solicitation of Potiphar's wife, his intentions were good. But the consequences of his actions would seem to contradict the "morality" of his choice. In his case, he is both moral, "good intentions," and immoral, "bad consequences." How can one be expected to deal with so confusing a concept?

The New Moralist, then, is one who claims to have the solution for the dilemma faced by the person who does not want to be a legalist but also does not want to be lawless. He says that you can bring no preset code of laws or rules to any decision-making situation—no law, that is, except the law of love.

WHAT'S WRONG WITH THE NEW MORALITY?

What are the shortcomings of the New Morality?

1. *It promotes a confusing concept of love.* Since love is the absolute of the New Morality, and since each moral decision must be measured by this concept, one would expect a very clear definition of love. But Carl Henry, the former editor of *Christianity Today,* is right when he observes that "love" is a word batted to and fro like a shuttlecock in Fletcher's *Situation Ethics.*[10] Graham B. Blaine, Jr., points out that "it is the deep confusion about love that makes the new morality virtually useless as a system of ethics."[11]

How confused are these "moralist theologians"? Dr. John Lachs, professor of philosophy at the College of William and Mary, shows how unsure Fletcher is about the meaning of love by citing no less than ten different definitions of love in Fletcher's book *Situation Ethics.* Says Fletcher, it is (1) "An action or a way of behaving" (p. 61); (2) "A characteristic of certain human actions and relationships" (p. 63); (3) "The motive behind the decision to act" (p. 155); (4) "An attitude of persons" (p. 79); (5) "A disposition to act in certain ways" (p. 61); (6) "A preference for certain values" (p. 104); (7) "Good will or a conative predisposition to take certain attitudes" (p. 105); (8) "A relation" (p. 105); (9) "A formal principle" (p. 60); (10) "A regulative principle" (p. 61).[12]

The New Testament language distinguishes three types of love: agape, phileo, and eros. Agape love is the highest form of love. It belongs exclusively to God and is given by Him to His children as a free gift of grace. By definition, agape love seeks only good for the one loved. Agape love willingly sacrifices itself for the sake of the loved one. Agape love is characterized by giving (see John 3:16; Eph. 5:25). It is this kind of love that is commanded of all believers (see Matt. 22:34-40; Rom. 5:5; Gal. 5:22; Eph. 5:2, 25).

Phileo love is a "fondness, affection, or liking for another." It is the love of friendship and feelings. It is emotional love (see John 11:3, 36; 1 Pet. 1:22).

The Greek term for eros love is not found in the New Testament. In the Greek language, it refers to love based in passion. We get our English word "erotic" from this root concept. Eros is passion seeking satisfaction. Eros is attracted by the satisfaction its object brings.

Though the New Morality claims to love with the kind of agape love that Jesus exalts in Matthew 22:34-40, a careful examination shows that the love of the New Morality is closer to eros love, that is, feelings that result from the satisfaction and pleasure (primarily sexual) obtained from the love object.

If the concept of love is the key to the New Morality, and if this concept is unclear in the minds of the leading scholars of the movement, how can they offer a working solution to anyone's real problems?

2. *It places man in control instead of God.* St. Augustine summarized the philosophy behind the New Morality when he wrote, "Love with care and then what you will, do."[13] On the surface, Augustine's instruction sounds noble. The problem, as we have already noted, is in the great latitude that is granted in interpreting love. The loving action for one person

becomes an unloving action for another. Each person comes to a situation with his own value system and does what he thinks is loving and right. In essence, morality is reduced to personal preference.

This is what was going on in the days of the Old Testament judges: "Every man was doing that which was right in his own eyes" (Judg. 21:25). Notice that the Bible does not say they did wrong, but rather that every man did what was right as he saw it. Man became his own God, which was nothing less than secular humanism in its purest form.

Harvard sociologist David Reisman says that this amnesia about God and neighbor is making American life brutish, as is the cult of self-expression: "Letting it all hang out and being candid are viewed as virtues, and this leads to rudeness." Columbia psychologist Jonathan Friedman roots the "me first" attitude in economic pressures, political frustrations, and unrealistic expectations of happiness through affluence: "The upshot may be less concern for how your actions affect others."[14]

By nature, people are more concerned about themselves and the satisfaction of their own needs and desires than about anything else. The Bible says all men are sinners and, consequently, cannot be trusted to do the right and loving thing. A code of behavior that says only "Do whatever you wish, but act lovingly and hurt no one" will inevitably operate to the satisfaction of one's own appetites, needs, and desires, and to the harm of others.

Carl Henry, while editor of *Christianity Today,* wrote:

When the individual is left wholly to himself to decide what legitimate forms his love for his neighbor might take, he soon and often becomes a tyrant toward his neighbor, the victim. When love has not been codified in binding law, the lover himself becomes the law. The new moralists naively fail to recognize that in a world in which there is no list of sins and every man is left to himself to decide whether incest, murder, adultery, or any other act is right or wrong, his neighbor has no defense or protection against any form of evil. . . . In the attempt to avoid legalism, the new morality deprives every man of all protection of his neighbor's exercise of love without law. . . . If the new morality were widely adopted, civil law would lose its moral basis to bring any man to trial for his deeds. If no conceivable human action is per se immoral and sinful, if there is no prescriptive ethics, if no one but the person himself can decide in his own situation whether any act is right or wrong, there is no moral basis for prosecuting any man at law for any act he might commit.[15]

3. *It paints an unrealistic picture of biblical Christian morality.* Joseph Fletcher calls the Christian who takes the Bible as the inspired Word of God a "legalist" who is too immature and childish to want to operate with real freedom to make moral decisions.[16] Dr. Paul Lehman, another "new morality advocate," calls the old morality "absolutist ethics," which he defines as "a standard of conduct which can and must be applied to all people in all situations in exactly the same way."[17]

Fletcher paints Christian moralists as weak-minded people whose lives are controlled by fear. He uses an anonymous poem to illustrate his belief:

> There was a young lady named Wilde
> Who kept herself quite undefiled
> By thinking of Jesus
> And social diseases
> And the fear of having a child.

For the New Moralist, the Bible is interesting reading and an example of the ethical achievements of men during the first century, but the mature "Christian" has grown beyond its truths. But Christian morality is not a "childish," absolutist ethic that lives its whole life out of fear. The biblical principles of morality are timeless truths that will guide any willing follower through the maze of moral decisions, even the tough ones.

Any debate can be won on paper by constructing an opponent of one's own choosing and then soundly defeating him. If, however, we are interested in the truth, we will always reject this kind of philosophical dishonesty. Joseph Fletcher's "straw man," called legalism, is easily demolished, and it should be. But as Bible scholar Vernon Grounds points out, biblical morality—what the Bible really teaches about right and wrong—is not made of straw.

4. *It protects a "hidden agenda."* The hard truth is that while man may say that he wants to do the right thing, more often than not he has self-interest in mind. He uses his intellect to build an acceptable theology for the passions and practices of his life. G. K. Chesterton has said, "The Christian ideal has not been tried and found wanting; it has been found difficult and left untried."

One of the most powerful illustrations of the unstated motives of the New Morality is found in this statement by Peter Howard, a former reporter for the *Beaverbrook Press* in London:

> My generation at Oxford had a funny outlook. Aldous Huxley was one of our great heroes. We were absolutely determined that no one should tell us what to do. But we used our brains to tell our conscience and our heart that what we wanted was right. We succeeded. And some of us did something even more far-reaching. We got important jobs and used our Oxford-trained intelligence to kill the conscience of the nation in order to make the nation more comfortable for us to live in. I think that was pretty good dictatorship. But, of course, we did it in the name of liberty. Then Huxley grew older. This is what he said some years later in *Ends and Means:* "I had motives for not wanting the world to have a meaning, consequently assumed it had none, and was able without difficulty to find satisfying reasons for this assumption. For myself, as no doubt for most of my contemporaries, the philosophy of meaninglessness was essentially a matter of liberation. The liberation we desired was simultaneously a liberation from a certain kind of morality. We objected to the morality because it interfered with our sexual freedom."[18]

WHAT ABOUT THOSE "SPECIAL SITUATIONS?"

Are there not illustrations in the Scriptures of special circumstances in which moral laws are suspended? Some cite, for instance, the story of Abraham and Isaac as a classic example of a conflict of moral principles. Here, they say, is the moral law forbidding murder being suspended for a higher moral law. But the story of Abraham does not prove this position at all. God explicitly commanded Abraham to sacrifice his son. In doing so, God exercised His prerogative to suspend or even revoke a previous law He had given. We must also remember that even though Abraham intended to kill Isaac, God intervened and the act was not carried out.

Other passages are sometimes cited to show that lying is right under certain circumstances. God blessed the Hebrew midwives who lied to the king of Egypt (see Ex. 1:18-20). But the king apparently accepted their explanation about why they did not kill the male Hebrew babies. It is probable that Hebrew women bore children without the aid of midwives; the midwives were telling part of the truth. But even if their reply were totally false, there is no evidence that the lie was approved by God. A similar situation is that of Rahab, the harlot who told a lie when she hid the spies. Subsequently in Scripture, she is praised for her faith, not the lie she told (see Heb. 11:25; James 2:25). A study of such passages nowhere indicates that those who lie are not guilty because of some higher law.[19]

William Banowski has the right perspective on situations where we today might feel ourselves caught between two conflicting moral principles:

> The truly mature person will inevitably, if infrequently, find himself caught in situations where he must decide and face the lesser of two evils. The important thing to know is that when the necessary alternative is chosen, it does not, in the process, change in character from evil to good. . . . What must be made clear at this point is that the difference between Christian morality and situation ethics is the difference between the necessary evil that is evil and needs repentance, and the necessary evil that is paraded as a positive good.[20]

WHAT DIFFERENCE DOES IT MAKE?

The question is a crucial one for the future of our country. All history bears witness to the fact that there can be no public virtue without private morality. There cannot be good government except in a good society. And there cannot be a good society unless the majority of individuals are at least trying to be good people. This is especially true in a democracy, where leaders and representatives are chosen from the people, by the people. The character of a democratic government will never be better than the character of the people it governs. A nation that is traveling the low road is a nation that is self-destructing. It is doomed, sooner or later, to collapse from within, or to be destroyed from without. And not all its wealth, science and technology will be able to save it. On the contrary, a decadent society will use, or rather misuse and abuse, these very advantages in such a way as to hasten its own destruction.[21]

And Kyle Haselden, an outspoken critic of the New Morality, has pointed out that "the love and do as you please" ethic can actually be more dangerous and destructive than outright moral disobedience. If right and wrong are relative terms, then everything is up to personal and subjective opinions. What is right and loving for one person may be evil and wrong for another.[22]

When we examine the New Morality, what do we discover? We discover that the New Morality comes perilously close to being what the old immorality condones: "The great principles of good and evil, kindness and cruelty, generosity or selfishness, love or lust do not change because some confused bishop writes a book about it."[23]

BUT WHAT CAN WE DO?

In an article by Ivan Hill in *Leadership Magazine*, he listed five reasons for the pervasive breakdown in morality. As you read his list of reasons, ask your own heart if you are countering or contributing to the moral erosion in our country:

1. Many of us are personally involved in and are profiting by dishonesty.
2. Too many of us are apathetic. We are afraid to take positive steps to halt today's raging rip-offs.
3. We put the importance of having money ahead of everything else.

4. Too many of us seem content in the belief that so long as we, ourselves, observe reasonable ethical standards, we do not need to feel responsible for the conduct of others.
5. Too many of us simply do not believe that corruption is all that bad. We have lived with it so long that it is beginning to look all right to us.[24]

NOTES

1. Clare Boothe Luce, "Is the New Morality Destroying America?" *The Human Life Review*, Summer 1978, p. 8.
2. Ivan Hill, *Leadership Magazine*, September 1980, p. 11.
3. Quoted by Andrew Kuyyehaven, "And Devour Your Sons and Daughters," *Banner*, November 10, 1980, p. 6.
4. Joseph Fletcher, *Situation Ethics: The New Morality* (Philadelphia: Westminster, 1966), p. 124.
5. Ibid., p. 144.
6. Ibid., p. 77.
7. Ibid., p. 140.
8. Ibid., p. 124.
9. Ibid., p. 16.
10. Carl Henry, "God's Will for a Wayward Age," *Christianity Today*, December 22, 1967, p. 25.
11. Graham B. Blaine, Jr., *Youth and the Hazards of Affluence: The High School and College Years* (New York: Harper and Row, 1966), p. 123.
12. John Lachs, "Dogmatist in Disguise," *The Christian Century*, November 16, 1966, pp. 140, 41.
13. Paul Ramsey, "Deeds and Rules in Christian Ethics," *Scottish Journal of Theology-Occasional Papers*, 11 (1965), p. 17.
14. Willis Elliott, "Whatever Became of the Golden Rule?" *Christian Herald*, May 1980.
15. Carl Henry, "Love Without Law," *Christianity Today*, October 8, 1965, p. 33.
16. Joseph Fletcher, *Situation Ethics*, pp. 81ff.
17. Paul Lehman, *Ethics in a Christian Context* (New York: Harper and Row, 1966), p. 125.
18. Quoted by Norman Vincent Peale, *Sin, Sex, and Self-Control* (Garden City, N.Y.: Doubleday, 1965), p. 64.

19. Erwin Lutzer, *The Morality Gap* (Chicago: Moody, 1972), pp. 101, 102.
20. William S. Banowski, "The New Morality, A Christian Solution," *Campus Evangelism* (R. B. Sweet Company), pp. 13, 14.
21. Clare Boothe Luce, "Is the New Morality Destroying America?" p. 8. © 1978 by *The Human Life Review*. Reprinted with Permission.
22. Kyle Haselden, *Morality and the Mass Media* (Nashville: Broadman, 1968), p. 27.
23. Quoted by Arnold Lunn and Garth Lern, *The Cult of Softness* (London: Blanford, 1965), p. 12.
24. Ivan Hill, *Leadership Magazine*, p. 11.

CHAPTER

SIX

God Bless Our Home

Eternal Father, who hast given
To homes on earth foretaste of heaven,
Whose gentle Spirit from above
Doth breathe Thy peace in hearts that love;
    While here we bide, or far we roam,
    Hear this our prayer: God Bless Our Home!

O Saviour, who didst smile to see
The bridal feast in Galilee,
Whose grace we crave on all who bow,
For life and death to take their vow;
    While here we bide, or far we roam,
    Hear this our prayer: God Bless Our Home!

O Tender Shepherd, who dost hold
Each little lamb within Thy fold,
With rod and staff who followest still
The wandering sheep o'er vale and hill;
    While here we bide, or far we roam,
    Hear this our prayer: God Bless Our Home!

Eternal Father, ever near,
With arm outstretched and listening ear,
Whose mercy keeps, whose power defends
Our sons, our daughters, and our friends,
    While here we bide, or far we roam,
    Hear this our prayer: God Bless Our Home!

Robert Freeman

HAS GOD
CHANGED HIS MIND?

AS WE TURN to God's Word, the importance of the family is clear from almost the first chapter to the last. It is in God's mind and heart throughout every generation and dispensation!

> The Bible is the world's great teacher of monogamy—the union for life of one man and one woman in marriage as the basis of the family. Whatever may be said about the time of the writing of the books of the Bible, or parts of them, the testimony of the whole is incontrovertibly to the point that marriage springs from the choice of one man and one woman of each other for a permanent family relationship. Over and through the whole of the Bible this ideal is dominant. There may be instances shown here and there of violation of this rule. But such cases are to be regarded as contrary to the underlying principle of marriage— known even at the time of their occurrence to be antagonistic to the principle.[1]

Regardless of how the family is portrayed in God's Word, it is clear that God never ignores it; nor is there any indication that He ever planned to replace it with another form of communal living.

The charter for marriage given in the first two chapters of Genesis provides a foundation for marriage and the family and defines its purpose: "Be fruitful and multiply, and replenish the earth and subdue it" (Gen. 1:28). Genesis 2 further defines the purpose of marriage as companionship. After describing all of His creation as "good," God looked at man alone and said, "It is not good . . . I will make him a helper suitable for him" (Gen. 2:18 NASB). When God brought the woman to Adam, Adam called her "Eve," which means "The mother of all living."

This early picture of the family shows husband and wife, created in the image of God, living in fellowship with God and with each other. Together, they rule the earth, committed to their Creator and each other.

The words of the marriage charter support this ideal: "a man," "his wife." These words hold the sexes to monogamy. The following words make marriage permanent: "The twain shall be one flesh." Two become one. "Wherefore they are no more twain but one flesh" (Matt. 19:6).

Sin enters in Genesis 3, and at the root of that sin is the violation of the marriage formula, the husband in authority over his one wife. Dr. H. A. Kent points this out in his book *The Pastoral Epistles:*

> Thus the fall was caused, not only by disobeying God's command not to eat, but also by violating the divinely appointed relation between the sexes. A woman assumed headship, and man with full knowledge of the act, subordinated himself to her leadership and ate of the fruit (Rom. 5:19). Both violated their positions. Subordination of woman to man is not Paul's invention. It is rooted in the very nature of the sexes and was put there by God Himself. Disaster comes when the relationship is violated.[2]

Kent was right about disaster. One has only to survey the remainder of Genesis to see how quickly the violation of the family begins to multiply. Lamech becomes a polygamist (see 4:19). Ham looks upon the nakedness of his father (see 9:22). Abraham has an adulterous affair with Hagar (see 16:2). Homosexuality ravages Sodom (see 19:1-11). Lot commits incest with his two daughters (see 19:30-38). Abraham tempts Abimelech to lust after Sarah (see 20:1-5). Isaac shows preferential treatment for Esau (see 25:27-34). Isaac follows his father's bad example (see 26:6-11). Shechem rapes Dinah (see 34:1-5). Jacob follows Isaac's bad example by showing preferential treatment for Joseph (see 37:1-4). Judah commits adultery with Tamar, his daughter-in-law (see 38:1-19).

The rest of the early record of family life is punctuated with polygamous marriages, but never without bad consequence and never without disapproval: Abraham (see Gen. 26:34, 35; 28:8, 9); Jacob (see Gen. 29:30); Elkanah (see 1 Sam. 1:2); David (see 1 Sam. 25:42-44; 2 Sam. 5:13-16; 1 Chr. 14:3); and, of course, Solomon.

Though polygamy was never expressly forbidden in the Old Testament, a careful study of these and other polygamous marriages shows the unhappiness of such family life. Jesus certainly affirms monogamous marriage as He refers to Genesis in Matthew 19:3-6; yet only the relationship of Isaac and Rebeccah seems to champion the cause of monogamous marriage in the chapters that immediately follow the fall of man in the garden.

The Book of Genesis also makes statements about the importance of the family in less obvious ways; for instance, the genealogies (those Scriptures we usually pass over in our devotional reading) declare the value of the family as they drone out their message that lineage matters, descent is important, and continuity and identity are to be found in the family unit. In the record of the Flood, God brings family units into the ark for safety.

O. R. Johnston calls Genesis 11-50 the family chronicles and observes that this section of Scripture is "packed . . . to the very end with intensely personal records of family life . . . jealousy and hatred, betrayal and reverse, scheming and deception, as well as forgiveness, faithfulness and joy."[3]

The Book of Exodus begins with the record of the families who came into Egypt, "every man and his household" (Ex. 1:1). The story of the deliverance of these captive families, who in four hundred years had multiplied to over two million souls, is complete with the record of their preparation for departure. They were gathered together by families, and a lamb was provided for each family unit (Ex. 12:3).

Exodus also contains the Ten Commandments. The first four pertain to our relationship with God. The next six deal with human relationships, and of the six, three are intended to protect the family. The fifth commandment instructs children to honor their father and mother. The seventh commandment forbids adultery, providing the security of the home. (Whatever children are born are to be family-born. All sex outside the marriage union is seen as sin.) The tenth commandment forbids the coveting of that which belongs to one's neighbor, including his wife. This was obviously an Old Testament prohibition against mental lust. What Jesus taught in Matthew 5:27-28 was no new truth. These ten commandments are reiterated in Deuteronomy 5:16-21. Exodus also records the importance of family instruction in the form of dialogue between parents and children (Ex. 12:26; 13:14). This instruction seems to be informal rather than formal or structured.

Leviticus 20 contains God's family protection act. In this chapter, five anti-family practices are condemned: child sacrifice (vv. 1-5), adultery (v. 10), incest (vv. 11, 12, 14, 17-21), homosexuality (v. 13), and bestiality (vv. 15, 16).

Deuteronomy contains what someone has called the "textus classicus" for family teaching. Deuteronomy 6:7-9 says, "And you shall teach them diligently to your sons and shall talk of them when . . . you rise up. And you shall bind them as a sign on your hand and they shall be as frontals on your forehead. And you shall write them on the doorposts . . . and on your gates" (NASB). And Deuteronomy 6:2 says that these commandments are given "to thee, thy son, and thy son's son" (see also Deut. 29:29).

It is also in Deuteronomy that we find the first and foundational passage on divorce—Deuteronomy 24:1-4. This is the Scripture to which Jesus refers in Matthew 19, and it is the first and legal document in the Bible dealing with the termination of marriage. Divorce is also condemned in Leviticus 21:7; 22:13; Numbers 5:12-31; 30:9,10; Deuteronomy 22:19; and Malachi 2:14-16.

Throughout the rest of Old Testament history, we see many vignettes of family life: the father-son relationship of Abraham and Isaac (see Gen. 18:19); Gideon trying to force his son to be an executioner (see Judg. 8:18-21); Jephthah foolishly bringing judgment upon an innocent daughter (see Judg. 11:34-40); the entire story of the Book of Ruth; the failure of Eli to restrain his sons (see 1 Sam. 1:1-28); the punishment of David's children after his sin with Bathsheba (see 2 Sam. 13); the picture of

Job with his family (see Job 29:5, 18-20); and family units working together in Ezra and Nehemiah. It is also very evident that family life was important in the development of leaders such as Moses, Samson, Gideon, Samuel, and David.

The picture of the family in the rest of the Old Testament is largely restricted to the Song of Solomon, the Book of Proverbs, and a few isolated psalms. The Song of Solomon, though symbolizing the relationship of Christ to His church, was obviously written to describe the intimate love relationship between a man and his wife. It is an Old Testament commentary on Hebrews 13:4. "Marriage is honorable in all, and the bed undefiled." According to one author, "It is a dramatic poem which for its erotic frankness and realism, its unabashed exultation of loving sensualism, has few rivals in world literature."[4]

Psalm 45 describes the relationship between the king and his royal bride. Psalms 127, 128 are also psalms of the home. Psalm 127 is well known for its focus on children: "Behold, children are a gift of the LORD; the fruit of the womb is a reward. Like the arrows in the hand of a warrior, so are the children of one's youth. How blessed is the man whose quiver is full of them; they shall not be ashamed, when they speak with their enemies in the gate" (127:3-5 NASB).

Psalm 128 pictures the whole godly family together in peaceful and joyous fellowship: "Your wife shall be like a fruitful vine, within your house, your children like olive plants around your table. Behold, for thus shall the man be blessed who fears the LORD" (128:3, 4 NASB).

The Book of Proverbs is a practical handbook on many aspects of family life. Among other family topics, it addresses itself to the following:

- Discipline of children—13:24; 19:18; 22:15; 23:13; 29:15; 29:17; 3:1, 2; 10:5; 17:2; 19:20, 26; 23:24, 25.
- Family problems—11:29; 17:1; 28:24.
- Sexual deviations—22:14; 23:26-28; 29:3; 30:20.
- Adulterous women—2:16-19; 5:3-13; 6:32; 7:19, 20.
- The ideal wife—31:1-31.

- A man and his wife— 5:8-21; 18:22; 19:14; 21:9; 25:24; 27:15, 16.
- Education in the home—4:1-6; 22:6.
- Contentious wives—21:9; 25:24; 27:15, 16.
- Rebellious children—17:21; 20:20; 30:17.
- Parent-child relationships—1:4, 8; 6:20-29; 17:21; 20:20; 30:17.

The last words of the Old Testament provide a curious bookend to the family message. With a reference to Elijah who shall come, Malachi writes: "And he shall turn the heart of the fathers to the children, and the heart of the children to their fathers, lest I come and smite the earth with a curse" (Mal. 4:6).

When Zechariah the prophet foretells the happy days that are coming for his people, he sees those days as days for the family: "Thus saith the Lord of hosts; there shall yet old men and old women dwell in the streets of Jerusalem, and every man with his staff in his hand for very age. And the streets of the city shall be full of boys and girls playing in the streets thereof . . . and they shall live with their children, and turn again" (Zech. 8:4-5; 10:9). Clearly the Old Testament, from beginning to end, upholds the importance of the family. Though the information covers a time period of two thousand years, there is no indication that God changed His mind about the original blueprint given in Genesis 1-3. The family is just as important in Malachi's day as it is in the Garden of Eden.

As we approach the New Testament, we see the family unit composed of husband, wife, children, plus servants, dependent relatives, and voluntary adherents who joined the household by mutual consent as employees, friends, and so on.

In the Gospels, Jesus reaffirms the original charter of the family (see Matt. 19:1-12) but says very little else about the family. He came not to destroy the Law but to fulfill it, to fill it out and expand it. He did establish one tenet before unknown, namely, that marriage is an earthbound institution and is not perpetrated in heaven (see Matt. 22:30; Mark 12:25; Luke 20:24-36).

One of the first family pictures portrayed in the New Testament is the detailed account of the preparation for a birth of John the Baptist (see Luke 1:6-7, 25).

This is followed chronologically by the detailed account of Jesus' birth (see Luke 1:26-37; 2:5-7; 17; 18; 33-37). The significant role of the family is powerfully confirmed by realizing that Jesus Himself came into an earthly family and accepted the pattern of family living for thirty years (see Luke 2:40, 51, 52).

Edith Deen writes about the Lord's family life:

These years were His real preparation for the ministry. Though He knew the value of periodic retreats into solitude for prayer and meditation, and spent forty days alone in the wilderness after His baptism, His training took place, not among such semi-monastic groups as the Qumran community or the pious Essenes, but in the everyday round of family living, both in His own home and homes of friends. The word "family" never occurs in His teachings, but His emphasis on the family is everywhere evidenced—in His love of God the Father, in His reverence for motherhood, in His tenderness toward little children, in His many references to sonship and brotherhood, and in His love of home. In using the imagery of the family in these and other instances, Jesus struck the chords of hope and understanding with the ordinary people to whom He ministered, people among whom He lived all of His life.[5]

Our Lord's first miracle was performed at Cana of Galilee, where He turned the water into wine at a marriage feast (see John 2:1-11). Every time He is asked by a relative to heal or raise a son or daughter, He responds (see Mark 5:23, 35-43). During His earthly ministry, Jesus actually broke up three funerals: Jairus's daughter (see Mark 5; Luke 8:41-46); the widow's son (see Luke 7:12-15); Lazarus (see John 11:21-32). Each funeral was a family affair. His deep love for children is seen in passages such as Matthew 19:13-14 and Mark 10:13-16. As He hangs on the Roman cross in death, He cares for His mother so that she might be supported by an adopted son (see John 19:26).

The Book of Acts continues the family emphasis of the New Testament. Here we have the record of whole families coming to faith in Christ. Cornelius (see Acts 10), Lydia (see Acts 16), the Philippian jailor (see Acts 16), and Crispus (see Acts 18:8) all led their families in a conversion decision. According to Acts 5:42 and Acts 20:20, individualized instruction in the faith took place in each home.

Timothy's preparation for ministry was anchored in the home by a godly, believing mother (see Acts 16:1-3). Acts also introduces us to the first married ministry team, Aquila and Priscilla (see Acts 18:2, 26).

In Gene Getz's book on the family, he questions the paucity of actual family references in the Epistles. Only 4 out of 95 verses in Colossians speak to the family. Four separate statements are made:

3:18—Wives—submit to your husbands, as is fitting in the Lord.

3:19—Husbands—love your wives and do not be harsh with them.

3:20—Children—obey your parents in everything, for this pleases the Lord.

3:21—Fathers—do not embitter your children, or they will become discouraged.[6]

Ephesians elaborates on these statements, but still only 16 of the 155 verses are given over to the family. The other Epistles have scattered references to the family. The role of the single Christian is taught in 1 Corinthians 7. This same chapter speaks to the critical issue of sex in marriage. Chapter 9 of 1 Corinthians presents Paul and Barnabas as bachelors. Chapter 13 of 1 Corinthians is the primary chapter in the New Testament on the concept of agape love, the indispensable home ingredient. First Corinthians 14:24, 35 instructs the husband to be the teacher of his wife, and chapter 16 mentions the conversion of Stephanas and his household.

In the rest of the New Testament, five of Paul's letters (Romans, 2 Corinthians, Galatians, Philippians, and 2 Thessalonians) make no direct reference to the family whatsoever. First Thessalonians 2:7-11 employs an illustration from the home.

In 1 Timothy, Paul refers to the care of widows (see chap. 5) and cites the proper home life of leaders as a prerequisite to leadership (see 1 Tim. 3:4, 12). Here he also mentions that one of the marks of the end time deceivers is that they forbid people to marry (see 1 Tim. 4:3). Perhaps the most important reference to the family in the pastoral epistles, however, is 1 Timothy 5:8: "If anyone does not provide for his own, and especially for those of his household, he has denied the faith, and is worse than an unbeliever" (NASB).

Though most Christians assign this verse to the financial care of the family, there is little reason to believe that Paul is not also including the other aspects of family care, even the spiritual.

In Paul's second letter to Timothy, he refers to Timothy's home life (see 2 Tim. 1:5; 3:14, 15). Here he also lists disobedience to parents with the grossest of sins (see 2 Tim. 3:2).

Titus contains a brief additional reference to Timothy's home life and catalogs a curriculum for older women to follow in teaching the younger women in the church (see Titus 1:5; 2:4-5).

The writer of Hebrews refers to the home as he writes that "marriage is honorable in all, and the bed undefiled" (Heb. 13:4). James, Jude, and John make no specific mention of the family, though the apostle John certainly employs the language of the family as he communicates to the saints.

Only the third chapter of 1 Peter specifically treats the home. Second Peter and the Book of Revelation avoid any mention of this subject.

In comparison with the total volume of New Testament teaching about the church, the information on the home seems limited. Getz raises the question of why there is so little *direct* information in the Bible on the subject of the home. Why aren't larger portions of the New Testament devoted to this important institution? Why hasn't the Lord left us with more instructions? Getz's conclusion is that He has. In reality, an individual household in some instances was a local church, at least in its initial days (see 1 Cor. 16:15). The home was used for worship, because the early Christians were banned from worshiping in the synagogues, and they were forbidden by law from having their own buildings for worship. Therefore, we discover numerous references in the New Testament to "household churches" (see Rom. 16:3-5; 1 Cor. 16:19; Col. 3:15; Philem. 2).[7]

The impact of this historical setting is very significant. The church existed within the home, so what was written to the church was written to the home. Therefore, most of the New Testament can be applied directly to the family.

As we look back over our survey through the Scriptures for God's Word about the family, we discover that God has always put high priority on the family. Oscar Feucht summarizes the reasons:

> God planned the family. He made it the keystone in human living. It launches human beings into the world; it starts them out on their journey of life; it protects them in mind and body in their first perilous years and helps to develop in them the personality which they will have for life. Above all, the family is God's instrument to insert into people the life which they do not have by physical birth, the life which God Himself must give through His Spirit and because of Jesus Christ.[8]

So the answer to the big problems of the family does not rest in some new family form or structure. We will not begin to relieve the causes of family breakdown mentioned in the last few chapters until we get back to the original blueprint. The French scholar Von Allwen wrote:

> It is hardly likely that this Biblical picture of the Christian family depends essentially on the social conditions of the ancient world, for it is too deeply rooted in the doctrine of the fatherhood of God and the indissoluble unity there is between Christ and His church. If social conditions change, then it will be the church's task to discover in the new setting a form of family life where the core of Biblical teaching on the family can continue to flourish without altercation.[9]

But is there anything that you and I can do in these times to insure that the "core of Biblical teaching on the family can continue to flourish without altercation"? I believe there is.

First of all, we must be careful *never* to excuse behavior that violates the biblical norm. We have become so tolerant in our times that we have lost sight of God's ideal. It is right to be concerned about the pain of those who are living outside the boundaries of the revealed will of God, but our concern can breed compromise.

Second, we must be willing to stand up for the family no matter what the cost. My friends Tim and Bev LaHaye have paid dearly for their commitment to the family. They have been picketed, threatened, and harassed. Just this week as I write these words, some ERA supporters have painted hate slogans on the front of the church formerly pastored by the LaHayes. In huge letters were written these words, "Down with Tim and Bev," "We hate the ERA haters." An obscene note was left on the desk of the pastor's study inside the building. I know that this kind of personal attack is not easily dismissed.

It is tragic that *so few* are willing to stand on the front line in the battle for the family. This war will eventually be lost unless more of us get involved in the struggle. And as you explore the next section of this book, you will see that the battle for the family is nothing more nor less than the battle for our nation.

NOTES

1. *International Standard Bible Encyclopedia*, rev. ed., s.v. "Family."
2. H. A. Kent, *The Pastoral Epistles*, (Chicago: Moody, 1958), pp. 114,115.
3. O. R. Johnston, *Who Needs the Family?* (Downers Grove, IL: InterVarsity, 1979), p. 33.
4. Vernon Grounds, *The New Look in Ethics,* Part IV, "The Christian Case for Pre-Marital Continence," Unpublished Paper (Denver, CO: Conservative Baptist Seminary), p. 4.
5. Edith Deen, *Family Living in the Bible* (New York: Harper and Row, 1963), p. 29.
6. Gene Getz, *The Measure of a Family* (Glendale, CA: Regal, 1976), p. 11.

7. Ibid., pp. 12,13.
8. Oscar Feucht, *Helping Families Through the Church* (St. Louis: Concordia, 1960), p. 9.
9. *Vocabulary of the Bible*, s.v. "Family."

SECTION II:
THE
NATION

CHAPTER
SEVEN

No Nation Liveth unto Itself

Voices are crying from the dust of Tyre,
From Baalbec and the stones of Babylon:
"We raised our pillars upon self-desire,
And perished from the large gaze of the sun."

Eternity was on the pyramid,
And immortality on Greece and Rome;
But in them all the ancient traitor hid,
And so they tottered like unstable foam.

There was no substance in their soaring hopes;
The voice of Thebes is now a desert cry;
A spider bars the road with filmy ropes
Where once the feet of Carthage thundered by.

A bittern booms where once fair Helen
      laughed;
A thistle nods where once the Forum poured;
A lizard lifts and listens on a shaft,
Where once of old the Colosseum roared.

No house can stand, no kingdom can endure
Built on the crumbling rock of self-desire;
Nothing is living stone, nothing is sure,
That is not whitened in the social fire.

Author Unknown

HOW ARE THE
MIGHTY FALLEN?

MANY YEARS AGO, Thomas Macaulay, a British historian, made a very perceptive comment about our nation. This man died on the eve of our Civil War, back in the middle of the nineteenth century, and this is what he said:

> Your republic will be fearfully plundered and laid waste by barbarians in the twentieth century, with this difference: The Huns and the Vandals who ransacked Rome were from without, and your Huns and Vandals will come from within your own country, and be engendered from within by your own institutions.

Whether we know it or not, our nation seems bent on fulfilling Macaulay's prediction. We have allowed great inroads to be made into family life, and our national life has simultaneously decayed. The historian's prediction is especially frightening as we view today's scene.

Recently, I did an in-depth study of the Old Testament book of Daniel, which records the rise and fall of the kingdoms of the world, both prophetically and historically. There in the pages of a relatively brief book, one is able to trace the decline of a nation to its ultimate destruction. I watched as God's judgment fell on the nation of Babylon for her sin, and I could not help but notice the many parallels to our own land.

A PROSPEROUS NATION

The city of Babylon was a testimony to the wealth of the Babylonian people. It was a magnificent display of prosperity that would compare even today with the great cities of the world. The walls of the city were 387 feet high and 85 feet wide. They were so gigantic that chariots, four abreast, could be driven around the top of them.

The city itself was a perfect square, fifteen miles on each side. The city boasted wide streets and tremendous public buildings and was populated, believe it or not, by 1.2 million people. Around the exterior of the walls flowed a deep, wide moat. Through the city ran the mighty Euphrates River.

Gardens, palm groves, orchards, and farmland dotted the countryside, providing enough food to feed all the people of the city. In fact, had the Medes and Persians not used subterfuge to conquer Babylon, it might never have fallen. It is said that the Babylonians had stored enough food to feed the million plus inhabitants for over twenty years.

Within the city were gigantic shrines erected to the Babylonian deities. Their beauty was eclipsed only by the marvelous, hanging gardens that Nebuchadnezzar had built for his wife. The engineering technology used to construct this seventh wonder of the ancient world would rival much that is done today.

Babylon was to the ancient world what the United States is to today's. One has only to travel abroad briefly to realize that even the poorest Americans are considered prosperous to the majority of the world.

A PROUD NATION

One night as King Nebuchadnezzar strolled along the palace terrace, he looked out over the magnificent city of Babylon and, overwhelmed with pride and selfishness, his heart exploded into vain words: "Is not this great Babylon, that I have built for the house of the kingdom by the might of my power, and for the honor of my majesty?" (Dan. 4:30).

The personal pronouns of his statement drip with glory, pride, and pagan arrogance. This exaggerated and dishonest self-evaluation was the signal that brought God's judgment down upon his head. "Pride goeth before destruction, and a haughty spirit before a fall" (Prov. 16:18). Nebuchadnezzar learned that "God resisteth the proud" (James 4:6).

Others before him had made the same mistake. In fact, the very first sin was the sin of pride. The record of the fall of Lucifer from heaven is the record of a proud heart:

> How art thou fallen from heaven, O Lucifer, son of the morning! How art thou cut down to the ground, which didst weaken the nations! For thou hast said in thine heart, I will ascend into heaven, I will exalt my throne above the stars of God; I will sit also upon the mount of the congregation, in the sides of the north: I will ascend above the heights of the clouds; I will be like the most High (Isa. 14:12-14).

King Herod tried the same thing. His record is preserved for us in Acts 12:21-23:

> And upon a set day Herod, arrayed in royal apparel, sat upon his throne, and made an oration unto them. And the people gave a shout, saying, It is the voice of a god, and not of a man. And immediately the angel of the Lord smote him, because he gave not God the glory: and he was eaten of worms.

Victor Hugo gives us a more modern example in the account of Napoleon and the Battle of Waterloo. On the morning of the battle, the little dictator stood gazing upon the field of battle as he described to his commanding officer his strategy for that day's campaign: "We will put the infantry here, the cavalry there, the artillery here. At the end of the day, England will be at the feet of France and Wellington will be the prisoner of Napoleon."

After a pause, the commanding officer said, "But we must not forget that man proposes but God disposes."

With arrogant pride, the little dictator stretched his body to full height and replied, "I want you to understand, Sir, that Napoleon proposes and Napoleon disposes." Hugo went on to write, "From that moment, Waterloo was lost, for God sent rain and hail so that the troops of Napoleon could not maneuver as he had planned, and on the night of the battle it was Napoleon who was prisoner of Wellington and France was at the feet of England."[1]

While Nebuchadnezzar's arrogant words were in his mouth, a voice from heaven was heard and Nebuchadnezzar was immediately insane. He was inflicted with lycanthropy, a disease of the mind in which a man imagines he is a wolf. For seven years, the king who had conquered the whole earth occupied the palace grounds, eating grass like an ox.

Pride is, according to C. S. Lewis,

> the essential vice, the utmost evil . . . unchastity, anger, greed, drunkenness, and all that, are mere flea bites in comparison. It was through pride that the devil became the Devil. Pride leads to every other vice. It is the complete anti-God state of mind. A proud man is always looking down on things and people: and, of course, as long as you are looking down, you cannot see something that is above you.[2]

The Bible warns against many sins, but there is one that seems to get more attention than the others, and that is the sin of pride. It is on God's hate list (see Prov. 6:16-18; 7:17). According to Mark 7:20-23, pride is one of the sins that proceeds from the heart of man and corrupts him.

Pride is a distorted self-appraisal that God hates and that the Bible denounces. Solomon's proverbs are strong reminders to all people that God hates pride and will not let it go unpunished:

Proverbs 8:13—The fear of the Lord is to hate evil: pride, and arrogancy, and the evil way, and the froward mouth, do I hate.

Proverbs 11:2—When pride cometh, then cometh shame: but with the lowly is wisdom.

Proverbs 16:5—Every one that is proud in heart is an abomination of the Lord: though hand join hand, he shall not be unpunished.

Proverbs 16:18—Pride goeth before destruction, and an haughty spirit before a fall.

Proverbs 21:4—A high look, and a proud heart, and the plowing of the wicked, is sin.

Proverbs 29:23—A man's pride shall bring him low: but honor shall uphold the humble in spirit.

It is right and good to be patriotic. It is wrong and sinful to be proud. Almost everywhere I travel to speak across this nation, I run into people who reflect their proud hearts by speaking of the relative goodness of America. "No matter how evil we are," they say, "we are not as evil as Russia or China or _____."

I believe that the traumatic events of the past decade have been allowed by God as a rebuke to the pride of this nation. Who would have believed that "godly" America could have experienced the race riots, assassinations, and governmental corruption of our generation? There are many of us who believe that our present economic stress is one last attempt by God to get our attention.

For many years, God warned King Nebuchadnezzar. He had the testimony of Daniel's personal life for over thirty years. (There must have been times when the king thought God was tolerating his arrogant spirit.) But one day God had had enough, and He sent judgment. Solomon admonishes us, "Because sentence against an evil work is not executed speedily, therefore the heart of the sons of men is fully set in them to do evil" (Eccl. 8:11).

> Though the mills of God grind slowly
> Yet they grind exceeding small
> Though with patience He stands waiting
> With exactness grinds He all.

When God was through with this proud king, he had learned the lesson of humility. The final words of Nebuchadnezzar reflect the conviction of a lesson understood by bitter experience: "Now I Nebuchadnezzar praise and extol and honor the King of Heaven, all whose works are truth, and his ways judgment: and those that walk in pride he is able to abase" (Dan. 4:37).

I pray that America will not be reduced to "eating the grass" of subjection as a godless nation before she repents of her pride and again honors the King of heaven.

A PROFANE NATION

Twenty or thirty years after Nebuchadnezzar's reign, his grandson, Belshazzar, became Babylon's leader. Belshazzar was a wicked and profane man, and under his leadership,

Babylon was pushed to the ultimate in immorality and idolatry. The end came for Babylon on a night when the whole governmental establishment was involved in a drunken party.

According to Xenophon, the historian, the occasion was a great festival among the Babylonians to their god Bel. Modern archaeology has excavated the very banquet hall where this party was held. According to their findings, the room was 60 feet wide and 172 feet long.[3]

The sensuality of the feast is documented in the first four verses of Daniel 5, where we are told that the king drank with his lords and that the women were present at the party. It was a sign of lust and sensuality when the women were present at Babylonian parties. (see Esth. 1:1-9).

In the midst of this debauchery, Belshazzar remembers the holy vessels that were taken from Jerusalem when the first Jewish captives were brought to Babylon. He sends a slave to bring those sacred vessels to his party so that he might profane them by drinking wine to his heathen gods from them.

Charles Swindoll has described what happened at that point:

Shortly the slave arrived with the holy vessels at that raucous banquet room. The moment had arrived for this maggot of a man to do a God-defying act. The erotic dancing suddenly stopped. The musicians put down their instruments and the house lights were turned up.

Belshazzar took the goblet, filled it from his own private wine and smirking with arrogance slopped the crimson liquid to his lips. As it dribbled down his beard, he glares around with the, "There, I've done it," look, as if possessed by the devil he was honoring. "He has done it," a thousand gasped. Suddenly a cheer broke out, blasphemously applauding the daring act.

Belshazzar sank down in his elegant seat. The music and erotic dancing began again. Ah, at last, he felt like a man.[4]

Dr. Seis in his *Voices from Babylon* has written:

Not only their ill-timed merriment, their tromping on their customary propriety and their drunkenness, but even their foolhardy and blasphemous insult to the Most High God, is veiled over and cloaked up with a pretense of devotion. This was as far as it was possible for human daring and infatuation to go. It was more than the powers of heaven could quietly endure.[5]

As I write these words in our own profane society, the newspapers here on the West Coast have been filled with the story of a university professor who had been asking his students to get involved in all kinds of sexual experiences with each other and then write up those experiences and turn in their reports for credit. They were told they would get more credit if their experiences were homosexual or lesbian in nature. Of course, the professor set the example by having several sexual experiences with his students, men and women alike.

The depths to which this country has stooped in pornography and filth places it not far behind Babylon in profanity. Men laugh today when we tell them that our modern civilization is doomed, but I am certain that Belshazzar never conceived of his mighty empire being overthrown, either.

A PRESUMPTUOUS NATION

Perhaps the most sobering comparison between our land and ancient Babylon is the spirit of presumption. We are living through the "fortress America" syndrome in our country. With all our technology and scientific surveillance systems, we presume ourselves to be impregnable.

One of the most sobering experiences I have had as an American citizen took place a few months ago in Mexico. A staff couple from our church invited my wife and me to accompany them for dinner to a Mexican restaurant in Tiajuana. Though I am not a Mexican food enthusiast, I do love Mexico and was excited about our visit. After dinner, we decided to walk through the city and visit some of the shops.

As we moved toward the center of town, I began to hear a loud Spanish-speaking voice. We turned the next corner, and I saw something that sent chills up my spine. Large banners with the hammer and sickle emblem of Soviet Russia were flying everywhere. People were crowded into the street, where they listened to an articulate speaker "preaching" communism with the fervor of an evangelist.

The Spanish I had learned in college was enough to help me understand that these communist leaders were condemning "American imperialism" and urging the crowd to "put down capitalism" and raise the Soviet flag.

I stood in sad unbelief. This was happening less than fifty miles from my home. The security of my country seemed rather fragile at that moment as I remembered that one of communism's primary strategies is encirclement.

As frightening as that is, it is not nearly as disturbing as a letter I received recently from a national security organization that decried the apathy of congressmen and senators toward our national security. If their report is accurate, we have fallen seriously behind in our ability to defend our nation, and we have ceased to care enough to look at the evidence. While the liquor flows in Washington, our nation is in jeopardy.

There is reason to believe that part of the motivation behind Belshazzar's big palace party was his desire to make fun of the Medes and Persians who had besieged Babylon unsuccessfully for many days. The leaders of the "great nation" were reveling in arrogant drunkenness. They were untouchable. They were so well fortified that no enemy could get to them.

There is an old secular proverb that says, "Whom the gods would destroy, they first make mad." History reveals how stupid Belshazzar was to be partying on that night. It literally turned out to be his own funeral wake!

Now let Herodotus, the Greek historian, tell us exactly what took place on that fateful night:

> Cyrus . . . then advanced against Babylon. But the Babylonians, having taken the field, awaiting his coming, and when he had advanced near the city, the Babylonians gave battle, and, being defeated were shut up in the city. But as they had long been aware of the restless spirit of Cyrus, and saw that he attacked all nations alike, they had laid up provisions for many years, and therefore, were under no apprehensions about a siege.

On the other hand, Cyrus found himself in difficulty, since much time had elapsed, and his affairs were not at all advanced, whether, therefore, someone else made the suggestion to him in his perplexity or whether he himself devised the plan, he had recourse to the following stratagem.

Having stationed the bulk of his army near the passage of the river where it enters Babylon, and again having stationed another division beyond the city, where the river makes its exit, he gave orders to his forces to enter the city as soon as they should see the stream fordable.

Having stationed his forces and given these directions, he marched himself away with the ineffective part of his army; and having come to the lake, Cyrus did the same with respect to the river and the lake as the Queen of the Babylonians had done; for having diverted the river, by means of a canal, into the lake, which was before a swamp, he made the ancient channel fordable by the sinking of the river. When this took place, the Persians who were appointed to that purpose close to the stream of the river, which had subsided to about the middle of a man's thigh, entered Babylon by this passage. It is related by people who inhabited the city at the time that by reason of the great extent, when they were at the extremities, those Babylonians who inhibited the center, knew nothing of the capture (for it happened to be a festival), but they were dancing at the time and enjoying themselves.[6]

I am told by two men who were there that when the Japanese attacked Pearl Harbor, they waited until the Americans had received their paychecks and then they infiltrated the bars with their own people and bought free drinks to supplement the already heavy flow of booze. On Sunday morning, when most of the American servicemen were suffering from a hangover, they initiated their surprise attack.

BUT THE END CAME

While proud Belshazzar shook his fist in God's face, God Almighty dispatched one finger and wrote the doom of Babylon on the wall of the palace banquet hall. While the Babylonian leaders were sucking up their wine out of holy vessels from Jerusalem, God's patience ran out, and He wrote the death knell of Belshazzar.

The famous words written on the king's banquet room wall simply announced that God was through with Babylon. The kingdom was numbered and God was finished with it. Babylon had been weighed in the balance and found wanting. The kingdom would be divided and given to the Medes and Persians (see Dan. 5:25-28).

Behind the magnificent walls of Babylon, the king laughed at the approach of Cyrus. But God had determined the king's fate, and that night he was slain and the nation fell.

It is overwhelming to realize that the Scripture presents the passing away of the Babylonian Empire in but two verses of Scripture. The night was the sixteenth day of Tishri, 539 B.C. On that night, Babylon joined the whole host of nations that have forgotten God and fallen: the Hittites, the Egyptians, the Assyrians, the Medo-Persians, the Greeks, the Romans, the French, and the Germans, to name just a few.

John Walvoord concludes from his study of Daniel 5:

> The long chapter devoted to this incident which brought the Babylonian Empire to its close is undoubtedly recorded in the Word of God not only for its historic fulfillment of the prophecies relative to the Babylonian Empire, but also as an illustration of divine dealing with a wicked world. In many respects, modern civilization is much like ancient Babylon, resplendent with its monuments of architectural triumph, as secure as human hands and ingenuity could make it, and yet defenseless, against the judgment of God at the proper hour.[7]

Isaiah the prophet writes the epitaph of this once proud nation: "Babylon is fallen, is fallen; and all the graven images of her gods he hath broken unto the ground" (Isa. 21:9).

As you read these next chapters, let this "cry of a fallen nation" remind you that "the wicked shall be turned into hell, and *all the nations that forget God*" (Ps. 9:17, emphasis added).

NOTES

1. Quoted by Lehman Strauss, *Daniel* (Neptune, N.J.: Loizeaux, 1969), pp. 124, 125.
2. C. S. Lewis, *Christian Behavior* (New York: Macmillan, 1946), pp. 44-48.
3. John F. Walvoord, *The Key to Prophecy* (Chicago: Moody, 1971), p. 120.
4. From tape series on Daniel by Charles Swindoll.
5. Quoted in Phillip R. Newell, *Daniel* (Chicago: Moody, 1962), p. 64.
6. Herodotus *History of the Persian Wars* 1.190–191.
7. Walvoord, *The Key to Prophecy*, p. 131.

CHAPTER
EIGHT

The Jew

Scattered by God's avenging hand,
    Afflicted and forlorn,
Sad wanderers from their pleasant land
    Do Judah's children mourn;
And e'en in Christian countries, few
Breathe thoughts of pity for the Jew.

Yet listen, Gentile, do you love
    The Bible's precious page?
Then let your hearts with kindness move
    To Israel's heritage;
Who traced those lines of love for you?
Each sacred writer was a Jew.

And then as years and ages passed,
    And nations rose and fell,
Though clouds and darkness oft were cast
    O'er captive Israel,
The oracles of God for you
Were kept in safety by the Jew.

And when the great Redeemer came
    For guilty man to bleed,
He did not take an angel's name;
    No—Born of Abraham's seed,
Jesus, who gave His life for you,
The gentle Saviour was a Jew.

And though His own received Him not,
    And turned in pride away,
Whence is the Gentile's happier lot?
    Are you more just than they?
No; God in pity turned to you—
Have you not pity for the Jew?

Go, then, and bend your knee to pray
    For Israel's ancient race;
Ask the dear Saviour every day
    To call them by His grace;
Go, for a debt of love is due
From Christian Gentiles to the Jew.

Author Unknown[1]

DOES AMERICA HAVE A RESPONSIBILITY TO THE JEW?

FREDERICK THE GREAT of Germany was something of a skeptic because of his association with Voltaire, the French infidel. On one occasion he addressed his court chaplain with these words: "Give me proof that the Bible is a Divine Book."

His chaplain replied, "The Jew, your Majesty, the Jew."

It has been said that the story of Israel is the most fascinating story ever told. The history of the indestructible Jew—a miracle people—is recorded in a miracle Book—the Bible—and is the story of the nation through which came the miracle person—the Lord Jesus Christ.

Although the nation of Israel is comparatively small in number and limited in world influence, more space in the Bible is allotted to her and her relationship to God than to any other subject.

The Book of Genesis is a good example. Two chapters in Genesis are given to the whole story of Creation. One chapter is given to the record of the Fall. Eight chapters cover the whole history of the world from Creation to the time of Abraham. Then thirty-eight chapters deal with the life stories of Abraham, Isaac, and Jacob. To God, Abraham and his descendants are of great importance.

Mark Twain once wrote this about the Jews:

Jews constitute but one percent of the human race. It suggests a nebulous, dim puff of stardust in the blaze of the Milky Way. Properly the Jew ought hardly to be heard of, but he is heard of. He is as prominent on this planet as any other people. His commercial importance is extravagantly out of proportion to the smallness of his bulk. His contributions to the world's list of great names in literature, science, art, music, finance, medicine and abstruse learning are also altogether out of proportion to the weakness of his numbers. He has made a marvelous fight in the world in all ages and he has done it with his hands tied behind him.[2]

One interesting statement repeated three times in the Old Testament indicates how very special Israel is to God and demonstrates how he cares for and protects His people. In Deuteronomy 32:10 we read, "He found him in a desert land . . . He kept him as the apple of his eye." David, a Jew, prayed, "Keep me as the apple of the eye" (Ps. 17:8). In relation to Israel among the nations, God promised, "After the glory hath he sent me unto the nations which spoiled you: for he that toucheth you toucheth the apple of his eye" (Zech. 2:8).

Charles Feinberg helps us to understand what this means:

Remarkable and abundant provision is made for the protection of the eye. The protection consists of (1) the strong frontal bones to guard against a blow, (2) the brow and eyelash to protect against dust, (3) the lid to guard against glare, and (4) the tear gland to provide continuous cleansing. With Israel is the omnipotent power of God committed to protect them.[3]

That God has had His hand upon Israel is beyond question. People often wonder, however, why this is so. It is not because Israel is more in number than other people. Deuteronomy 7:6, 7 says,

For thou art a holy people unto the Lord thy God: the Lord thy God hath chosen thee to be a special people unto himself, above all people that are upon the face of the earth. The Lord did not set his love upon you, nor choose you, because ye were more in number than any people; for ye were the fewest of all people.

It is not because Israel was more sensitive to God than other nations. Isaiah 45:4 says, "For Jacob my servant's sake, and Israel mine elect, I have even called thee by thy name: I have surnamed thee, though thou hast not known me."

It is not because Israel was more righteous than other nations. When God was confirming His promise of land to the Jews, He said, "Understand, therefore, that the Lord thy God giveth thee not this land to possess it for thy righteousness; for thou art a stiff-necked people" (Deut. 9:6).

God had blessed Israel because in His sovereignty He chose to do so, and He confirmed His choice in the promise He made first to Abraham, the father of the Jewish nation. That promise is recorded in Genesis 12:1-3:

> Now the Lord had said unto Abram, Get thee out of thy country, and from thy kindred, and from thy father's house, unto a land that I will show thee. And I will make of thee a great nation, and I will bless thee, and make thy name great; and thou shalt be a blessing: And I will bless them that bless thee, and curse him that curseth thee: and in thee shall all families of the earth be blessed.

Basically, that covenant with Abraham promises three things that are of interest to us as we look at our nation's relationship with Israel.

1. A special blessing on any nation that will be a blessing to Abraham's descendants. ("And I will bless them that bless thee.")
2. A special curse on any nation that curses Israel. ("And curse him that curseth thee.")
3. A special universal blessing on all nations. ("In thee shall all families of the earth be blessed.")

These three provisions provide the basis for our attitude as Christian Americans toward the Jewish people.

AMERICA IS INDEBTED TO ISRAEL FOR HER SPIRITUAL HERITAGE

All the spiritual influences and moral forces that have in any way blessed and enlightened the world of humanity had their sources in the Hebrew nation.

1. The Hebrew people gave to the world the Ten Commandments and the Law that have largely been the basis of jurisprudence and statutory proceedings among the civilized nations of the world to the present day.

2. The Bible, the Word of God, was channeled through the Hebrew nation. This book has done more than all the other books ever written to bring the knowledge of the true God to

the people of the world and to lift them from the bondage and darkness of paganism. All of the known writers of the Bible were Jews, with the possible exception of Luke.

3. Jesus Christ, the world's Savior, was, according to the flesh, a Jew. The story is told of a Jewish lad who fell in the street under a shower of stones thrown by some haters of his race. A godly woman stepped into the street and helped the boy to his feet. With her handkerchief she wiped some of the blood off his face, planted a kiss on his forehead, and said, "God bless you my lad, my Savior was a Jew." Every born-again Christian can identify and should identify with this incident.

4. Christianity, with its message of grace and its uplifting influence for nearly two thousand years, was born in Jerusalem, nursed and cradled by the Hebrew nation. The Lord chose certain men to proclaim and explain His coming. Every one of those men was of the Jewish household of faith. We must also remember that the first martyrs of the Christian faith were Jewish: Stephen (see Acts 7:59, 60) and James (see Acts 12:1, 2). Our Lord spoke the truth when He said, "Salvation is from the Jews."

> Know ye therefore that they which are of faith, the same are the sons of Abraham. And the scripture, foreseeing that God would justify the heathen through faith, preached before the gospel unto Abraham, saying, In thee shall all nations be blessed. So then they which be of faith are blessed with faithful Abraham. . . . And if ye be Christ's, then are ye Abraham's seed, and heirs according to the promise (Gal. 3:7-9, 29).

A wealthy man once entertained a well-known minister in his home. "There's nothing Jewish in my house!" he boasted. "I have such a hatred for the Jew that I will have nothing Jewish in my house."

The minister quietly arose and took a beautifully bound Bible from the table and a New Testament from the bookcase and put them before the fireplace. He then went on to take down some paintings from the wall. He removed one picture of Paul preaching at Athens and another of the crucifixion.

The man was greatly surprised and asked, "What are you doing? Why are you taking such liberties in my house?"

To this the minister answered, "You just said that you would not have anything Jewish in your house. I was beginning to help you take away the many Jewish things you happened to have in this room. Shall I throw them in the fire?"

"Stop," the man cried, "May God forgive me. I have never thought of it in that light. Little did I know how greatly indebted I am to things Jewish."

Agnes Scott Kent has captured the contribution of the Jew in her Hebrew rendition of the recessional:

The Jewish Recessional

God of the ancient Hebrew race
  Lord of the Abrahamic line,
Illumine us that we may trace
Through Holy Writ Thy vast design.
  God of the Jew! Remind us yet,
  Lest we forget—lest we forget!

These are Thy Chosen People, Lord—
  In them all nations shall be blessed
When Israel, redeemed, restored,
Within the promised land finds rest.
  Thou hope of Zion, rouse us yet,
  Lest we forget—lest we forget.

To them adoption doth pertain,
  The covenants, the glory too:
The promises for aye remain;
The law was given—to the Jew.
  God of the fathers, guard us yet,
  Lest we forget—lest we forget.

The Holy Ghost moved men of old,
  And they, with far prophetic view,
God's great redemptive plan foretold:
The Book was written—by the Jew.
  Spirit of truth, O teach us yet,
  Lest we forget—lest we forget.

AMERICA IS INSTRUCTED BY THE WORD OF GOD TO BE A FRIEND OF ISRAEL

The warning to any nation that would mistreat Israel is clearly a part of God's covenant with Abraham: "And curse him that curseth thee" (Gen. 12:3). That truth is confirmed elsewhere in the Bible.

> The Lord shall cause thine enemies that rise up against thee to be smitten before thy face: they shall come out against thee one way, and flee before thee seven ways (Deut. 28:7).

> And the Lord thy God will put all these curses upon thine enemies, and upon them that hate thee, which persecuted thee (Deut. 30:7).

> Fear thou not; for I am with thee: be not dismayed; for I am thy God. I will strengthen thee; yea I will help thee; yea, I will uphold thee with the right hand of my righteousness. Behold, all they that were incensed against thee shall be ashamed and confounded; they shall be as nothing, and they that strive with thee shall perish. Thou shalt seek them, and shalt not find them, even them that contended with thee: they that war against thee shall be as nothing, and as a thing of naught (Isa. 41:10-12).

> Pour out thy fury upon the heathen that know thee not, and upon the families that call not on thy name: for they have eaten up Jacob, and devoured him, and consumed him, and have made his habitation desolate (Jer. 10:25).

> Therefore all they that devour thee shall be devoured; and all thine adversaries, everyone of them shall go into captivity; and they that spoil thee shall be a spoil, and all that prey upon thee will I give for a prey (Jer. 30:16).

> Thine hand shall be lifted up upon thine adversaries, and all thine enemies shall be cut off (Mic. 5:9).

When God spoke through His prophet Zechariah about the Day of the Lord, He said, "Then shall the Lord go forth, and fight against those nations, as when he fought in the day of battle" (Zech. 14:3).

My father told me about a preacher friend of his who, during World War II, announced as a sermon theme, "How to Destroy the Jew." The people crowded into that evening service because they feared the annihilation of the Jews by Hitler. The preacher's text was Jeremiah 31:35-37:

> Thus saith the Lord which giveth the sun for a light by day, and the ordinances of the moon and of the stars for a light by night,

who divideth the sea when the waves roar; the Lord of hosts is his name. If those ordinances depart from before me, saith the Lord, then the seed of Israel also shall cease from being a nation before me for ever. Thus saith the Lord; If heaven above can be measured, and the foundations of the earth searched out beneath, I will also cast off all the seed of Israel for all that they have done, saith the Lord.

It is as impossible to get rid of the Jew as it is to pull the sun from its orbit. It is as impossible to move the Jew out of his place as it is to move the planets out of their spheres. It is as impossible to prevent the Jew from coming to the ultimate end and place that God has for him as it is to shake the heavens and move them out of their ultimate habitation.

Yet, in spite of these warnings from the Word of God, the history of the Jews is the history of persecution. The attitude of many of the nations of the world is summarized by the words of the psalmist: "Come, and let us cut them off from being a nation; that the name of Israel may be no more in remembrance" (Ps. 83:4).

Pharaoh of Egypt devised a plan to destroy all the Hebrew male children born to Hebrew women, but God saw to it that the infant emancipator of His people would be concealed in the very place of death, the Nile River. Years later, Pharaoh and his soldiers paid for their anti-Semitism as they suffered death in a watery grave.

Under the Persian Empire, Satan-inspired Haman, the wicked favorite of King Ahasuerus, devised a scheme to destroy every Jew in the empire and bring a vast sum of money into the king's treasury. But he failed to realize that the death sentence would include the king's favorite wife, who was a Jewess. God had strategically placed her there for such a time as that. Haman's plan failed, and he was executed on the gallows he had prepared for the righteous Mordecai. Antiochus Epiphanes in the second century before Christ became one of Israel's unrelenting enemies, but in the end he, too, was defeated in his efforts to annihilate the Hebrews.

Herod tried to destroy Jesus by putting to death all the infants in Bethlehem. But once again, God interceded and our Jewish Redeemer was spared.

Hitler determined to destroy all the Jews on the European continent. He was filled with Satan and his fury. Those who knew him well reported that he would often stay up all night before a major campaign to commune with the spirit world. It is not hard to guess at the character of the spirits he consulted.

So great was Hitler's persecution of the Jews in Europe that the Jewish population of the world was reduced to probably less than the number of Jews who left Egypt under Moses. In Germany in 1938, within a few days, almost six hundred synagogues were destroyed. The windows of every Jewish establishment had been shattered. In the Buchenwald concentration camp, the death rate was 30 percent of the inmates. Similar conditions prevailed in Sachsenhausen and Dachau. The Auschwitz camp was equipped to execute 10,000 Jews per day. Treblinka, another of Hitler's torture camps, could destroy 25,000 per day. In the infamous Buchenwald camp, Jews were shipped and tortured during the day, while during the night a voice shouted over the loudspeakers, "Any Jew who wishes to hang himself is asked first to put a piece of paper in his mouth with his number on it so that we may know who he is."

Jacob Presser, in his book *The Destruction of the Dutch Jews,* describes what took place in Auschwitz after the Jews were unloaded from the train:

> This was the heartless "It's-time-to-take-a-shower" routine. Usually women and children were taken first. All were ordered to undress in a common room. Clothes had to be neatly folded and shoes tied together (these would be sent to non-Jews thought to be worthy by the Third Reich).
>
> The gas chamber appeared to be a shower room. To add reality to the lie, those entering were given a piece of soap and were promised a cup of coffee after the shower. When the room was packed with Jews, the forbidding door was shut and the gas was turned on. Within fifteen minutes the gruesome charade was over and it was time for the scavangers to begin their work. Gold teeth were removed. Wedding rings were taken off dead fingers. Women's hair was cut off. And the corpses were shoved into the ovens. The ritual was repeated again and again with the unfeeling efficiency of an assembly line. The end products were ashes and the few remaining possessions of European Jews who had already been robbed and uprooted.[4]

The infamous Adolf Eichmann expressed Nazi hatred for the Jews. He said, "I shall leap into my grave, for the thought that I have five million human lives on my conscience is to me a source of inordinate satisfaction."[5] The prediction of Moses concerning the Jews was literally fulfilled during these days.

> And the Lord shall scatter thee among all people, from one end of the earth even unto the other. . . . And among these nations shalt thou find no ease, neither shall the sole of thy foot have rest: but the Lord shall give thee there a trembling heart, and failing of eyes, and sorrow of mind. And thy life shall hang in doubt before thee; and thou shalt fear day and night, and shalt have none assurance of thy life: In the morning thou shalt say, Would God it were evening! And at evening thou shalt say, Would God it were morning! For the fear of thine heart wherewith thou shalt fear, and for the sight of thine eyes which thou shalt see" (Deut. 28:64-67).

According to a conservative estimate, over 6 million Jews were killed by Hitler's Gestapo; yet out of that mass slaughter the nation of Israel was born and lives today.

In June 1967, Israel was confronted with an Arab army of 653,000 men, 2,700 tanks, 1,090 war planes, and 205 ships. To meet this great force against them, Israel had 300,000 men, 800 tanks, and 19 ships. In spite of the insurmountable odds, the indestructible Jew survives!

Dr. C. J. Scofield was right when he wrote, "It has invariably fared ill with the people who have persecuted the Jew." Ask Egypt, Syria, Babylon, Rome, Spain, Germany, and Russia. They will testify to the reality of Dr. Scofield's statement.

The Christian attitude toward the Jew is stated well in the following poem "Christian and Jew" by Will Houghton.

> Say not a Christian e'er would persecute a Jew;
> A Gentile might, but not a Christian True.
> Pilate and Roman guard that folly tried,
> And with that great Jew's death, an empire died.
> You read a Bible passed to you with age;
> A Jew wrote this and that, and each succeeding page.
> The Book where Moses had so much to say,
> That Law he gave, makes statute books today.
> The poet sang of shepherd's care so kind,

Your mother found that Psalm a solace to her mind.
Ah, David wrote for her far better than he knew,
"The Lord My Shepherd,"—written by a Jew.
When Christians gather in Cathedral, Church or hall,
Hearts turn towards one—The name of Jesus call.
You cannot persecute—whatever else you do,
The race who gave Him—Jesus was a Jew![6]

One of the reasons America has been blessed is that she has become a homeland for the Jewish people. It has been predicted that by 1990 there will be 4.2 million Jews residing in Israel. But as early as 1970, the Jewish population in America had reached the 6 million mark and composed 3 percent of the population of the United States. Here the Jews could retain their religion and have economic, social, and educational opportunities. Today the Christian church in America stands firmly between the Jew and the repetition of any further anti-Semitism.

America was the first nation to recognize the new state of Israel in 1948. America was the first nation to appoint an ambassador to Israel. James G. McDonald was that man. America also assured Israel of a $1 million loan to enable the government to get on its feet. Unquestionably, the future of America and God's blessing upon her continues to depend upon her attitude toward the Jew. In this generation when we can ill-afford to risk any of God's blessing upon us, we do well to reconsider our policy with Israel. Political blunders and military compromise that endanger Israel also endanger America.

But America's responsibility to Israel in general and to the Jew in particular goes far beyond our national alliance with her. A prominent Jewish rabbi said recently, "We have given the world their religions, but have none ourselves. The people of Israel need Christ and, like the twelve whom Jesus sent out, we are to go to the lost sheep of the house of Israel" (see also Matt. 10:5-7).

When the great apostle Paul declared the truth of the gospel, he said, "For I am not ashamed of the gospel of Christ; for it is the power of God unto salvation to every one that believeth, to the Jew first, and also to the Greek" (Rom. 1:16).

Over a quarter of a century ago, a learned Russian Jew was sent to Palestine by the Jews to buy land for them. One day while in Jerusalem, he went up on the Mount of Olives to rest. Someone had told him to take a New Testament as the best guidebook for Jerusalem. The only Christ he had ever known was the Christ of the Greek and Roman churches, who were his persecutors and the persecutors of his people. As he read the New Testament, he became acquainted with the real Christ of whom the Old Testament Scriptures had foretold, and his heart grew warm. He looked off toward Calvary and he thought: *Why is it that my people are persecuted and cast out?* And his conviction gave the answer: *It is because we have put to death our Messiah.* He lifted his eyes to that Messiah and said, "My Lord and my God."

He came down from the mount a disciple of the Lord Jesus Christ. He went home to Russia and erected a synagogue for the Jews, over the door of which was written: "Let all the house of Israel know that God hath made this same Jesus whom ye have crucified, both Lord and Christ."

It is that message that Israel needs today. Who will take it to them if the Christians in America do not? Truly, "a debt of love is due, from Christian Gentiles to the Jew."

NOTES

1. Quoted by Robert L Evans, *The Jew in the Plan of God* (New York: Loizeau), pp. 141, 142.
2. Walter B. Knight, *Knight's Treasury of Illustrations* (Grand Rapids, MI: Eerdmans, 1963), p. 188.
3. Charles Feinberg, *Israel at the Center of History and Revelation* (Portland, OR: Multnomah, 1980), p. 42.
4. Jacob Presser, *The Destruction of the Dutch Jews* (New York: Dutton, 1969), p. 486.
5. Ibid., p. 336.
6. Will H. Houghton, "Christian and Jew," quoted by Robert L. Evans, *The Jew in the Plan of God* (New York: Loizeaux), p. 138.

CHAPTER
NINE

Three Things

I know three things must always be
To keep a nation strong and free.
One is a hearthstone bright and dear,
With busy, happy loved ones near.
One is a ready heart and hand
To love, and serve, and keep the land.
One is a worn and beaten way
To where the people go to pray.
So long as these are kept alive
Nation and people will survive.
God keep them always, everywhere—
The home, the heart, the place of prayer.

Author Unknown

IS THE CHURCH SEPARATE FROM THE STATE?

ONE OF THE most revolutionary truths ever to fall from the lips of Jesus Christ were these: "Render therefore unto Caesar the things which are Caesar's; and unto God the things that are God's" (Matt. 22:21). In that one statement He defined our relationship to the two great structures that have challenged the love and loyalty of people through the ages.

The quest for political and religious liberty drove the first European settlers to this land. Here they established what had not been known in their mother country, the opportunity to worship God according to the dictates of their own con-sciences.

When the First Amendment to our Constitution was written, it established this right for every American citizen. It reads: "Congress shall make no law respecting the establishment of religion or prohibiting the free exercise thereof."

Today, multiplied millions of every faith and race benefit from the priceless privilege secured to us by the "Separation of Church and State" amendment. History has demonstrated the damage that is done when Caesar attempts to control the church or when the church tries to control Caesar. As Christians, we have a responsibility both to the state and to God. We dare not ignore either. The Christian's highest goal is a free church in a free state.

It was Daniel Webster who said, "Whatever makes men good Christians, makes them good citizens." A man cannot be a good Christian who is not a good citizen. It is axiomatic that people cannot enjoy the privileges of liberty without assuming commensurate responsibilities.

Because of my first birth, I am a citizen of the United States of America, and because of my second birth, I am a citizen of the Kingdom of God. Both involve very serious obligations.

My responsibilities as a citizen are carefully spelled out in the Word of God. First, I am to pay the taxes that are due my government (see Matt. 22:17-21). For the record of Christ's paying tribute, see Matthew 17:24-27.

Second, I am to be subject to my government, recognizing that the government is ordained of God. Therefore, to resist the government is to resist God. "Render therefore to all their dues: tribute to whom tribute is due; custom to whom custom; fear to whom fear; honor to whom honor" (Rom. 13:7). The only exception to this principle is the application of Acts 5:29, "We ought to obey God rather than men" (see also Titus 3:1).

Third, I am to pray and give thanks for all those in authority with a view to a godly and honest life lived in quietness and peace (see 1 Tim. 2:1, 2).

Fourth, I am to obey the ordinances of man, whether the federal or state laws are in question. By so doing, I can silence the ignorance of foolish men (see 1 Pet. 2:13-17).

There are other biblical principles in the Old Testament that have some bearing on our responsibility to government (see Ex. 22:28; Ezra 6:10; 7:26; 10:8; Prov. 16:14, 15; 24:21; 25:6, 7; 25:15; Eccl. 8:2-4; 10:4; 10:20; Jer. 29:7).

A representative of the Roman Empire visiting the province of Palestine shortly after the death and resurrection of Christ reported to the emperor that those calling themselves Christians were characterized by two things, namely, "They sing songs and pay their taxes."

Christians must not resist the government's attempts to uphold morality and restrain evil in our society. However, when the government seeks to control or legislate against the interests of the church, Christians must stand against such activity:

These demands take a multitude of forms: attempts to control church nurseries, the various religious uses of church buildings, zoning regulations, etc. Christian schools are told that they must pay unemployment compensation, seek accreditation by the state, use state textbooks, teach humanism and so on. Catholic orders and protestant missionary agencies are told that they must pay unemployment compensation also. The National Labor Relations Board seeks to unionize parochial and Christian teachers and so on and on. Now, too, there is a demand that Christian schools be integrated at a percentage set by the Internal Revenue Service, this despite the fact that such schools have not been involved in segregation.[1]

The influence of the government in church and religious endeavors is being felt widely. Big government appears ready to dole out money to willing religious organizations. Many who for years complained about Roman Catholic churches and schools accepting the taxpayer's money to support and build their cause now seem ready to admit that everyone is doing it and that without federal help, they can't survive.

My college-president father, who for twenty-five years refused federal aid to a needy and growing college, drummed into my head this clear axiom: "The source of the money is the source of control." If we do not want the federal government telling us what to teach in our Christian schools and colleges, we had better ask God to show us how to finance our programs without government help.

I believe that the greatest safeguard to my religious freedom is the First Amendment to the Constitution. I believe wholeheartedly in the separation of the church and state, but I do not believe in the great illusion of that doctrine, which, when reduced to its least common denominator, insists that God be eliminated from government. Here is an explanation of what the Founding Fathers had in mind:

Justice Story's construction of the First Amendment has been corroborated by others. In the words of James Madison, the First Amendment religion clauses were prompted because the people feared one sect might obtain a pre-eminence, or two combine together and establish a religion to which they would compel others to conform. The concern of Madison and the Founding Fathers was that one Christian denomination might prevail over the others. Thus, the First Amendment was not meant to prevent the "establishment" of Christianity as a religion but to prevent a single Christian denomination from dominating all the rest. The framers had no intention of eradicating traditional theism via the First Amendment, because to them, religion entailed a relationship of man to a Supreme Being. . . . . History is replete with the close connections between the public institutions of this country and the religious policies of traditional Christian theism. The predominantly Christian orientation of the American people mitigates against the absolute separation of church and state. It is these facts that the framers had in mind when they drafted the First Amendment.[2]

Though the Founding Fathers wished to secure the religious freedom of all men, it was never their desire to create a secular, humanist nation with God uninvolved in her affairs.

It was Arnold Toynbee who said, "Democracy is another leaf from the book of Christianity, which has also, I fear, been torn out, and while, perhaps not misread, has certainly been half-emptied of meaning by being divorced from its Christian context and secularized."

But the extent to which we as Christians should attempt the integration of Christianity and citizenship has always divided good men. John Witherspoon struggled with that issue back in 1776. As a minister of the Gospel and the president of Princeton Seminary, he felt strongly that the church should not become entangled in civil affairs. "When our blessed Savior says, 'My kingdom is not of this world,' [as] he once preached, he plainly intimates to His disciples that they have no title to intermeddle with state affairs."

But when he was urged to serve as a delegate to the 1776 Continental Congress, Witherspoon, an astute Christian citizen, finally accepted the call. History records that it was his voice, as much as anyone's, that turned the tide of debate that tense, hot July 4 in Carpenter Hall. His resounding speech at a critical hour united the delegates in common conviction to pick up the pen and sign the Declaration of Independence.[3]

Roger Williams is often given credit for a strong stand against the state's intervention in the affairs of the church. Many, however, are not aware that Roger Williams's career was probably as political as the careers of those who expelled him from Massachusetts in 1636.

In the spring of 1636, Williams bought land from the Narangansett Indians on which he founded the city of Providence and the colony of Rhode Island. In 1643, he received a royal charter for Providence Plantations, and from 1654 to 1657, he served as president of the United Colonies of Rhode Island and Providence Plantations. In 1675, Williams was a captain of soldiers defending Providence against attacking Indians in King Phillip's war. He remained active in politics until his death in 1683.

Williams was consistent in upholding his belief in church-state separation, even while involved in politics. His argument with the Massachusetts authorities was that the state must not establish a uniform code of worship.[4]

Reading through the documents that formed the foundation of our nation, I was struck with the consistent appeal to an Almighty God as the source of strength and blessing. In 1606, before they left England, the settlers who founded the Jamestown colony wrote the First Charter of Virginia, which became the Constitution of the first settlement in this country. In that historic paper they dedicated themselves by the "providence of Almighty God," to the task of "propagating the Christian religion to such people as yet live in darkness." We are told that when they first stepped foot on shore of this land in April 1607, they erected a cross and held a prayer meeting.

When the pilgrims signed the Mayflower Compact on November 11, 1620, they pledged themselves in the name of God and for the glory of God to advance the Christian faith. Governor William Bradford reported that when "they were brought safe to land, they fell upon their knees and blessed the God of Heaven."

The first Constitution actually drafted in the United States was the fundamental orders of Connecticut, written in 1639. Among other things, it pledged its signers "to maintain and preserve the liberty and purity of the gospel of our Lord Jesus which we now profess."

The first confederation of the various communities of New England cited as the purpose for coming to America, "to advance the Kingdom of our Lord Jesus Christ and to enjoy the liberties of the gospel in purity and peace." During the formation of our Constitution in the late 1780s, Benjamin Franklin gave what is now a famous acknowledgment of God's sovereignty in the affairs of men:

> I have lived, sir, a long time, and the longer I live, the more convincing proof I see of this truth—that God governs in the affairs of men. And if a sparrow cannot fall to the ground without His notice, is it probable that an empire can rise without His aid? We have been assured, sir, in the sacred writings, "that except the Lord build the house, they labor in vain that build it." I firmly believe this; and I also believe that without His concurring aid we shall succeed in this political building no better than the builders of Babel.

During that same Continental Congress that met to establish the United States, there was a disagreement among representatives that threatened to break up the very union of the States. Benjamin Franklin broke in: "Mister President, I therefore move that henceforth prayers imploring the assistance of heaven be held in this assembly every morning." And every day since, Congress has begun with prayer. It was my honored privilege on November 7, 1979, to stand in the Senate Chamber as the guest chaplain of the Senate and continue the godly tradition that Benjamin Franklin initiated as I opened the Senate that day in prayer.

When George Washington delivered the first inaugural address on April 30, 1789, he said, "It would be peculiarly improper to omit in this first official act my fervent supplications to the Almighty Being who rules over the universe, who presides in the councils of nations." From that day until this, president after president without exception has made references or appeals to the aid of Almighty God in his inaugural address.

When he issued the first thanksgiving proclamation, Washington said, "It is the duty of all nations to acknowledge the providence of Almighty God, to obey His will, to be grateful for His benefits and humbly implore His protection and favor." John W. Whitehead and John Conlan have observed:

> Early American law was no less theistic in its configuration. Probably the greatest influence on the law as understood by the men responsible for formulating the foundations of the American legal system was William Blackstone's commentaries. Regarding the basis of law, Blackstone wrote: "The doctrine thus delivered we call the revealed or divine law, and they are to be found only in the Holy Scriptures . . . upon these two foundations, the law of nature and the law of revelation, depend all human laws. That is to say, no human laws should be suffered to contradict these."[5]

Overwhelming evidence of this acceptance of the divine basis of all government is found in all fifty state constitutions, which, without exception, contain an appeal or a prayer to the Almighty God of this universe.

Even our government buildings witness to our reliance on God and His Word. For instance, the Ten Commandments hang over the head of the Chief Justice of the United States Supreme Court. In the House and Senate chambers appear the words, "In God we trust." In the rotunda is the figure of the crucified Christ. On the walls of the Capitol dome these words appear, "The New Testament according to the Lord and Savior Jesus Christ." In the cornerstone of the Capitol building is a manuscript in the handwriting of Daniel Webster that concludes with these words,

> And all here assembled, whether belonging to the public life or, to private life, with hearts devotedly thankful to Almighty God for the preservation of the liberty and happiness of the country, unite in sincere and fervent prayers that this deposit, and the walls and the arches, the domes and the towers, the columns and the entablatures, now to be erected over it, may endure forever. God save the United States of America.

In the White House, where our president lives, over a fireplace are these words placed there by John Adams, the first president to inhabit the mansion: "I pray heaven to bestow the best of blessings on this White House and on all that shall hereafter inhabit it."

On the walls of the staircase of the Washington Monument are written the following individual phrases: "God and our native land"; "The memory of the just is blessed" (Prov. 10:7); "Search the Scriptures"; "Holiness to the Lord"; "Suffer the little children to come unto me and forbid them not; for of such is the kingdom of God"; "Train up a child in the way he should go: and when he is old he will not depart from it"; "In God we trust"; "May heaven to this union continue its beneficence." On the outside of the top of the monument is a metal cap on which are written these words: "Praise be to God."

On the various walls of the rooms of the Library of Congress are to be found the following words: "The heavens declare the glory of God; and the firmament showeth His handiwork"; "Wisdom is the principal thing; therefore get wisdom, and with all thy getting, get understanding"; "What doth the Lord require of thee, but to do justly, and to love mercy, and to walk humbly with thy God"; "One God, one element, and one far-off divine event, to which the whole creation moves"; "Nature is the art of God"; "That this nation under God, shall have a new birth of freedom, that government of the people, by the people, for the people, shall not perish from the earth."

Added to the evidence of the early documents and the inscriptions on our buildings are the inspiring words of our national anthem:

> Praise the power that hath made and preserved us a nation!
> Then conquer we must, when our cause it is just;
> And this be our motto: 'In God is our trust'
> And the star-spangled banner in triumph shall wave
> O'er the land of the free, and the home of the brave.[6]

Yes, the Bible does say, "Render unto Caesar the things which are Caesar's; and unto God the things which are God's." But that only applies to those things that government can legitimately require of us, that do not violate biblical instruction. That same Bible says, "Blessed is the nation whose God is the

Lord; and the people whom he hath chosen for his own inheritance" (Ps. 33:12). "Righteousness exalteth a nation: but sin is a reproach to any people" (Prov. 14:34). "The wicked shall be turned into hell, and all the nations that forget God" (Ps. 9:17).

Today the historic doctrine of separation of church and state is being violated by government agencies' intervention in the religious institutions of our country.

In Francis Schaeffer's *Christian Manifesto,* he included a list of thirty-one issues pending before United States' courts, administrative bodies, executive departments, and legislatures. These issues represent the growing determination of our government to control our lives. Among other questions, they include:

- Is a minister of the gospel liable for malpractice to a counselee for using spiritual guidance rather than psychological or medical techniques?
- Can HEW require a Bible college to admit drug addicts and alcoholics as "handicapped persons"?
- Can parents who send their children to religious schools not approved by a state board of education be prosecuted under the truancy laws?
- Can seminary trustees refuse to graduate a practicing homosexual?
- Must a religious school accept as a teacher an otherwise qualified practicing homosexual?
- Can a state department of health close a church-run juvenile home for policies that include spanking?
- Is an unborn fetus a "person" entitled to constitutional protection?
- Can a state official seize a church's assets on allegations of misconduct by dissident members and run the church through a court-appointed receiver?
- Can the state set minimum standards for private religious school curricula?
- Should churches be taxed like any other part of society?[7]

Along with this government intervention, there is the greater danger of eliminating the recognition of God and the influence of righteousness in matters of public life. Only history will reveal the cost of our having divorced God from government.

Some time ago, I read the following story. A shepherd in the hills of Idaho was a faithful radio listener to one of the finer musical programs on the air. One night after listening to the concert, he wrote a letter to the radio station in which he made a most unusual request. The letter said, in part:

> I enjoy your program from Los Angeles every week, and I am writing to ask you a favor. It's rather lonely up here in the hills, and I haven't much to entertain me except listening to the radio. I have an old violin which I once could play, but it has gotten badly out of tune. I wonder if you would take just a moment on your program next week to strike "A" on the piano, so that I may tune my violin again.

At first they smiled about that letter. But they honored the request, and when the program came on the air, they interrupted it long enough to strike "A" on the studio piano in Los Angeles, while the shepherd in the hills of Idaho got the right pitch for his violin.

Today America is out of tune. She has lost pitch by removing God from public life. It is time for individual Christians and evangelical churches to sound a clear "A."

NOTES

1. R. J. Rushdooney, *Chalcedon Report,* quoted by Homer Duncan, *Secular Humanism* (Lubbock, TX: Missionary Crusader, 1980), p. 48.
2. John W. Whitehead and John Conlan, "The Establishment of the Religion of Secular Humanism and Its First Amendment Implications," *Texas Tech Law Review,* vol. X, no. 1 (1979), pp. 2-5.
3. *Moody Monthly,* May 1980, p. 21.
4. Eric E. Wiggin, "Political Action—A Proper Response to Developments of our Time," *Baptist Bulletin,* May 1980, p. 8.

5. John W. Whitehead and John Conlan, "The Establishment of the Religion of Secular Humanism," pp. 25, 26.

6. Most historical and architectural references are contained in an unpublished pamphlet by D. James Kennedy under the title, "The Christian Foundations of American History."

7. Robert L. Toms, *Theology, News and Notes,* December 1980, pp. 18, 19, quoted by Francis Schaeffer, *A Christian Manifesto* (Westchester, IL: Crossway Books, 1982), pp. 83-85.

CHAPTER
TEN

A Nation's Strength

What makes a nation's pillars high
And its foundations strong?
What makes it mighty to defy
The foes that round it throng?

It is not gold. Its kingdoms grand
Go down in battle shock;
Its shafts are laid on sinking sand,
Not on abiding rock.

Is it the sword? Ask the red dust
Of empires passed away;
The blood has turned their stones to rust,
Their glory to decay.

And is it pride? Ah, that bright crown
Has seemed to nations sweet;
But God has struck its luster down
In ashes at his feet.

Not gold but only men can make
A people great and strong;
Men who for truth and honor's sake
Stand fast and suffer long.

Brave men who work while others sleep,
Who dare while others fly—
They build a nation's pillars deep
And lift them to the sky.

Ralph Waldo Emerson

IS WAR EVER IN
THE WILL OF GOD?

ONE OF THE great masterpieces of all time is Edward Gibbon's *The Decline and Fall of the Roman Empire*. The thesis of that survey of ancient Rome is this, "That it fell, not because of the superior enemy on the outside but because of the decay of Rome on the inside." Rome was not murdered, she committed suicide.

It was the Vandals, German barbarians, who came down out of the north and east of Europe and ravaged a great circle around the Imperial City—Gaul, Spain, North Africa, finally Carthage. In A.D. 455, they crossed over the narrow bridge from Carthage to Sicily to Italy itself.

While that desperate invasion was taking place, the young men of Rome sat in the stadium watching the games and declared what in their day amounted to, "Hell, no–we won't go." And the barbarians invaded and burned the city and put much of the population to the sword, then carried off the remainder into captivity and spoiled all the treasures of the great capital of the Roman Empire.

Recent newspaper stories about the resumption of registration for the draft report there will be upwards of 500,000 men who will either fail to hear of their responsibility to register or will refuse to do so. Another prediction is that as many as 50 percent of the eligible men, if called into the service, would respond, "Hell, no—we won't go."

War has been the history of man. From the day that Cain killed his brother, Abel, to this present hour, men have engaged in the slaughter of one another. It is estimated that during the past 5000 years, men have fought in over 14,000 wars. From

141

1496 B.C. to A.D. 1861, the world knew 3,130 years of war and 227 years of peace. In the last 400 years, European nations have entered into more than 8000 treaties of peace. They were all intended to be permanently binding. They lasted on the average for only two years.

In the First World War, 8,538,315 men and women gave their lives in the war that was to end all wars. In the Second World War, 22,000,000 of the world's citizens were offered on the altar of war. Our most recent war in Vietnam cost us 47,000 of our young men and maimed 100,000 additional men for life.

But the two World Wars of this century and the conflicts in Korea and Vietnam have been overshadowed by an even more significant event. On August 6, 1945, the first atomic weapon to be used in war was dropped on Hiroshima; three days later a second bomb was dropped on Nagasaki. Those three summer days heralded the opening of a new era in human history. Someone has called it the age of human omnipotence, for, unlike the omnipotence of God, man's omnipotence lies in his ability to destroy all living things in less than six days.[1]

Today the nuclear buildup is a horrendous reality. Each Poseidon submarine has 10 missiles, each of which has 14 MIRV warheads, each of which is equivalent to the Hiroshima bomb. So one submarine carries enough power to destroy 140 Hiroshimas. America's 11,000 nuclear warheads could annihilate the complete world population 12 times over.[2]

The United States Congress published a document called *The Effects of Nuclear War* in 1979. That document says that "the minimum consequences would be enormous." It provides four case studies ranging from a single megaton weapon attack on a city the size of Detroit or Leningrad to "a very large attack against a range of military and economic targets" in which the Soviety Union struck first and the United States retaliated. The former would mean 2 million dead and the latter up to 77 percent of the American population (about 160 million) and up to 40 percent of the Russians. Many more millions would die later of their injuries or starve or freeze to death the following winter, and cancer would claim many more victims.[3]

Can this be the will of God? How can a God who commands us to "love your enemies" and whose sixth command in the

Decalogue is "thou shalt not kill" allow for war in His economy? Many sincere Christians continue to wrestle with their personal responsibility in relation to military service. What help can we find in the Scripture? In the Old Testament, the Hebrew word *milhamah,* "war," occurs more than three hundred times. And *milhamah* is only one of several Hebrew words associated with the various facets of war. More than two hundred times in the Old Testament, Jehovah is called "the Lord of Hosts" (armies). After Moses and the Children of Israel escaped the clutches of Pharaoh through the intervention of Jehovah, they sang this song of victory: "The Lord is a man of war: the Lord is his name. Pharaoh's chariots and his host hath he cast into the sea" (Ex. 15:3).

Many of God's great servants were military men: Saul, David, Moses, Gideon, and many of the kings of Israel. Joshua, servant of the Lord and successor to Moses, was chosen by the Lord to lead His people Israel as they occupied the land of Canaan. They were told to exterminate the inhabitants of Canaan, and Jehovah promised His cooperation (Deut. 7:17-24).

God gave King Saul this command concerning Amalek, "Thus saith the Lord of Hosts . . . go and smite Amalek, and utterly destroy all that they have, and spare them not; but slay both man and woman, infant and suckling, ox and sheep, camel and ass" (1 Sam. 15:2,3).

The sons of Reuben, the Gadites, and half the tribe of Manasseh were helped against their enemies, "for they cried to God in battle, and he was entreated of them; because they put their trust in him. . . . For there fell down many slain, because *the war was of God* (1 Chr. 5:20-22, emphasis added).

This was the testimony of King David: "Blessed be the Lord my strength, which teacheth my hands to war, and my fingers to fight" (2 Sam. 22:35; Ps. 18:34; 144:1).

The laws of war given to the Israelites stipulated that when they fought against the "cities of these people, which the Lord thy God doth give thee for an inheritance, thou shalt save alive nothing that breatheth: But thou shalt utterly destroy them" (Deut. 20:16-18).

Dr. Peter C. Craigie, in his book *The Problem of War in the Old Testament,* argues for pacifism but has to admit that given this Old Testament view of God, his case is not as clear-cut as he would wish.[4]

The point is often made by the pacifists that while the Old Testament is full of war, it is scarcely mentioned in the New Testament. No one would argue that there is not more war in the Old Testament than in the New. There is a reason for that, however. In the Old Testament, we have the story of a nation that is to produce a Savior, while in the New Testament we have the story of the individuals who have accepted that Savior. The one is national, the other is spiritual. The one is collective, the other individual. If God were writing a third Testament today, it would be full of wars because the world is now getting ready for the coming of a Judge and a King.

But let us not pass over the New Testament so quickly. Wherever in the New Testament a soldier appears in the record, he appears in commendation and appreciation. In Luke 3:14, we have the record of the Roman soldiers coming to John the Baptist and repenting, "saying, And what shall we do? And he [John] said unto them, Do violence to no man, neither accuse any falsely; and be content with your wages." "Do violence to no man" is more accurately translated, "Extort from no man." John instructed these soldiers not to extort food and money from those who lived near military camps. That was a common practice among soldiers. "Be content with your wages" referred to the soldier's military service. John did not object to a man's serving as a soldier.

Five Roman centurions appear in the New Testament record, and all of them are presented favorably. In Matthew 8:5, we have the record of the centurion's coming to Christ in Capernaum and beseeching the Lord concerning his servant who was sick. When the Lord offered to come and heal him, the centurion said that if He, the Lord, would just speak a word, that would be enough. And the Lord said, "I have not found so great faith, no, not in Israel" (Matt. 8:10).

The centurion who, under Roman orders, helped with the crucifixion of Christ is the second example: "When the centurion, which stood over against him, saw that he so cried out, and gave up the ghost, he said, Truly this man was the Son of God" (Mark 15:39).

Three centurions appear in the Book of Acts. *Cornelius* is described as a devout man, one who feared God with all his house, gave much alms to the people, and prayed to God always. When his prayers came up for a memorial before God, God sent Simon Peter to him, and he became the first convert among the Gentiles (see Acts 10:1). *Claudius Lysias* appears on the scene in Acts 23. He is used as the instrument of God to save Paul from certain death at the hands of the Jews. *Julius,* a centurion in one of Augustus's divisions, saved Paul from the Roman soldiers who were going to kill him and the other prisoners on the grounded ship. "But the centurion, willing to save Paul, kept them from their purpose" (Acts 27:43).

The Roman soldiers were evangelized by Paul and later became evangelists themselves (see Acts 21:34, 37; 23:35). Paul said that his bonds in Christ were manifest in all the palace and in all other places (see Phil. 1:13).

Among the signs of the last days given by our Lord are "wars and rumors of wars" (Matt. 24:6; Mark 13:7; see also Luke 21:9). Jesus accepts war as part of the world order and draws from it an impressive illustration of the exacting conditions of Christian discipleship. "What king, going to make war against another king, sitteth not down first . . ." (Luke 14:31-33). He laments over Jerusalem because of the armies that will encompass her and the war that shall overcome her (see Luke 19:41-44). He conceives of Himself as having come not to send peace on earth, but a sword (see Matt. 10:34). He declares that they who take up the sword shall perish by the sword (Matt. 26:52).

The apostles use the terminology of war to describe the selfishness and greed of men. "From whence come wars and fightings among you? Come they not hence, even of your lusts that war in your members?" (James 4:1). They see, speaking figuratively of fleshly lusts, enemies that war against the soul. "Dearly beloved, I beseech you as strangers and pilgrims, abstain from fleshly lusts, which war against the soul" (1 Pet. 2:11). They find in war apt figures of the spiritual struggle and divine protection and ultimate victory of the Christian. It is the "law in my members, warring against the law of my mind, and bringing me into captivity to the law of sin" (Rom. 7:23).

Through Jesus Christ, we can become "conquerors" (Rom. 8:37). "Though we walk in the flesh, we do not war after the flesh" (2 Cor. 10:3). We are to bring "into captivity every thought to the obedience of Christ" (2 Cor. 10:5). Timothy was encouraged by Paul to "war a good warfare" (1 Tim. 1:18). We are caused "to triumph in Christ" (2 Cor. 2:14). Of Jesus Christ it is said that "having spoiled principalities and powers, he made a show of them openly, triumphing over them in it" (Col. 2:15).

But why does God allow war? What is the purpose of it, anyway? The Bible is clear on this point. God uses governments as vehicles to convey judgment upon nations that need it. Listen to the words of Paul in Romans 13:2-4:

> Whosoever therefore resisteth the power, resisteth the ordinance of God; and they that resist shall receive to themselves damnation. For rulers are not a terror to good works, but to the evil. Wilt thou then not be afraid of the power? Do that which is good, and thou shalt have the praise of the same. For he is a minister of God to thee for good. But if thou do that which is evil, be afraid; for he beareth not the sword in vain: *for he is the minister of God, a revenger to execute wrath upon him that doeth evil* (emphasis added).

The Old and New Testaments are filled with illustrations testifying to the fact that human governments are ordained of God. For example, in Daniel's time Nebuchadnezzar, a tyrant almost as wicked as Adolf Hitler, was ruler. Yet Daniel said of him, "The God of heaven hath given thee a kingdom, power, and strength, and glory. And wheresoever the children of men dwell, the beasts of the field and the fowls of the heaven hath he given into thine hand, and hath made thee ruler over them all" (Dan. 2:37, 38). "He removeth kings, and setteth up kings" (Dan. 2:21). When Pilate asked Jesus, "Knowest thou not that I have power to crucify thee, and have power to release thee?" Jesus answered, "Thou couldest have no power at all against me, except it were given thee from above" (John 19:10,11). When Paul wrote that "the powers that be are ordained of God" (Rom. 13:1), he was suffering Nero's tyranny.

And God often uses wicked nations to judge nations that have known the advantage of His blessing. The Bible says of wicked Pharaoh, "Even for this same purpose have I raised thee up, that I might show my power in thee, and that my name might be declared throughout all the earth" (Rom. 9:17).

The Book of Isaiah records that the Assyrians came down from the north to be the hand of God's judgment upon Israel: "O Assyrian, the rod of mine anger, and the staff in their hand is mine indignation" (Isa. 10:5). Habakkuk the prophet wrestled in his book with God's use of the Chaldeans to judge Judah. He wrote, "Wherefore lookest thou upon them that deal treacherously, and holdest thy tongue when the wicked devoureth the man that is more righteous than he?" (Hab. 1:13).

It is this truth more than any other that ought to strike terror into the heart of every American. We of all nations have been blessed of God, but we have so violated that blessing that we are now ripe for the judgment of God upon us. And God will not hesitate to use the godless Russians as the rod of His anger against us. There has never been a time in her history when America has been so vulnerable as she is today.

We have lost our will to defend our own nation. Oswald Spengler warned us that this would be the case. In his book *The Decline of the West,* he stated, "World peace involves the private renunciation of war on the part of the immense majority, but along with this, it involves an unavowed readiness to submit to being the booty of others who do not renounce it. It begins with the state destroying the wish for universal reconciliation, and it ends in nobody moving a finger so long as misfortune touches only his neighbor."[5]

Our present situation is very similar to that of Great Britain prior to World War II, when that country ignored the Nazi buildup and dismissed the warnings of Winston Churchill, who later called World War II "the unnecessary war." England, after World War I, just as this country after the Vietnam War, had an intense revulsion against war. It felt it had slaughtered its youth senselessly. Britain condemned itself, as American does today. The will to fight and defend its allies disappeared.[6]

While we have lost our will to fight, our adversary, the Soviet Union, has been preparing for war. Harvard's *Russian Research Center* has concluded that the Soviets believe they can fight, win, and survive a nuclear war. *The House Armed Services Committee* has reported that our strategic position has deteriorated so greatly that we now are unable to deter a first strike by Russia. *The Stockholm International Peace Research Institute* has warned that the probability of nuclear war is "steadily increasing . . . is virtually inescapable." The *Intelligence Digest of England* has concluded that the most probable time for the Russians to be militarily aggressive is within the next three to five years. The *Foreign Affairs Research Institute* of London has revealed that there is no parallel to the present Soviet buildup since that of Nazi Germany in the 1930s. The Soviets have enough food stored underground to feed their population for a year. They have a massive civil defense effort. Early in 1973, Brezhnev, in a speech to East European Communist Party leaders in Prague, Czechoslovakia, said that by 1985, the Soviet Union would be militarily and economically strong enough to exert its will anywhere in the world. Many believe that deadline has since been revised to 1982.[7]

General Lewis W. Walt, in his book *The Eleventh Hour,* warns:

> If someone in the Kremlin decided at this moment to push the nuclear button, there is nothing your government could do to save the lives of you and your loved ones. Within fifteen to thirty minutes, thermonuclear warheads, thousands of times more powerful than the bomb that ruined Hiroshima, would be raining down on our Minuteman Missile Sites, our strategic bomber bases, and on our cities. The lucky would be incinerated in the fireballs the diameters of which would be measured in miles, or in the fire storms which would roll across the states. Within a matter of hours, somewhere between sixty million and a hundred million men, women and children would die. The unlucky would be left to seek some bare existence in a poisoned and desolate landscape in which few traces of civilization would remain. The United States would be finished forever as a nation.[8]

What shall we do? Shall we begin to strengthen our defenses? Certainly, absolutely. America should have learned by now that baring our population to the Soviet sword has not promoted peace. While we were cutting back, they were building up, until today they have the world's most extensive air defense and civil defense systems. As much as we may be concerned about the buildup of nuclear arms, we must also realize that the only hope we have of survival, humanly speaking, is to be as strong as or stronger than our enemy. Someone has aptly said that prizefighters and linebackers don't get mugged.

The longest era of peace the world may have ever known, the celebrated *Pax Romana*, was made possible by the military strength of the Roman Empire. Nobody likes to think about war, but the fact of the matter is that the way *not* to have war is to be so strong that no other nation will dare attack. Years ago, during the Vietnam War, a GI helicopter pilot was killed, and on his tombstone in New Hampshire his parents had these nineteenth century words of John Stuart Mill inscribed:

> War is an ugly thing, but not the ugliest of things. The decayed and degraded state of moral and patriotic feeling, which thinks nothing is worth a war, is worse. A man who has nothing which he cares more about than his own personal safety is a miserable creature, and has no chance of being free unless he is made free and kept so by the exertions of better men than himself.

Shall we reinstitute the draft? Certainly. America should have learned by now that a volunteer army converts 60 percent of the defense dollar into recruitment costs, attracts less-educated personnel, and turns our once disciplined armed forces into a band of mercenaries.

But our real defense as a nation rests in the spiritual convictions, character, and commitment of our citizenry. David discovered that fact and declared: "Some trust in chariots, and some in horses: but we will remember the name of the LORD our God" (Ps. 20:7). It was God who said, "If my people, which are called by my name, shall humble themselves, and pray, and seek my face, and turn from their wicked ways; then will I hear from heaven, and will forgive their sin, and will heal their land" (2 Chr. 7:14). That verse reminds us that the work of God in our land must begin with us who are the people of God. We must return and repent and put our trust again in the God of our salvation. We must restore prayer to our lives, our homes, our churches, and our schools. We must remember from whence we are fallen: we must realize that while building a strong military, our trust must ultimately be in God. The danger of total faith in our military defense apart from God is as great as the danger of a second-rate military. The following poem summarizes well our need to depend on God.

> Where is the God of our fathers; the God of America's birth?
> The God that we once believed sovereign, and maker of heaven and earth?
> We now have found us some new gods, which we worship and serve as a slave;
> For the God of the Bible's forgotten in the land of the free and the brave.
> What power has the God of the Bible to offer this nuclear age?
> What help can He offer His people, in the Third World War they may wage?
> So all of you bow to the new gods, our brilliant new missile array.
> Trust only our arsenal rockets, our salvation by night and by day.
> And if you should use these murderous gods, which you trusted for your salvation,
> You may find that you only have sealed the curse of your own damnation.
> So America trust in your missiles, and forget that Jehovah is true.
> But be not surprised at the Judgment, If your God can't remember you.

A few years ago, our country welcomed a management consultant, as it were, who brought with him all his historical and philosophical tools and background. He observed our "eat, drink, and be merry" attitude. He noted the reckless debt assumption on the part of the consumer, the spending for things as if there were no tomorrow. He watched a decadent, legalistic society, operating on the cold letter of the law, which had lost its sense of justice and mercy. He told us the next war might well bury Western civilization forever. He concluded that we had lost our concept of a supreme, complete entity, a God, which formerly restrained our passions and irresponsibility. His name was Alexander Solzhenitsyn.

My position as a Christian American must be to work hard

for a strong country capable of defending itself against any military aggression. At the same time I must pray for peace, peace that can be won without compromising the godly principles that made this land great. And all the while I am doing these things, I must keep an eye on the future, realizing that the only real and lasting peace will come when the Prince of Peace returns to set up His kingdom on earth. "Come, behold the works of the Lord, what desolations he hath made in the earth. *He maketh wars to cease unto the end of the earth.* . . . Be still and know that I am God: I will be exalted among the heathen, I will be exalted in the earth" (Ps. 46:8-10, emphasis added).

The Prince of Peace is coming, earth's rightful Lord and King,
He'll still the warring nations, and truth and justice bring,
No other one can do it, and cause the longed-for peace;
He, He alone is able, "He maketh wars to cease."
Earth, cursed so long and troubled by passion, greed, and crime,
Shall yet be filled with Glory in that blest coming time;
Its tumult waxeth louder, its groans and pains increase,
But He is coming shortly, "He maketh wars to cease."

NOTES

1. Peter C. Craigie, *The Problem of War in the Old Testament* (Grand Rapids, MI: Eerdmans, 1978), p. 18.
2. John R. W. Stott, "Calling for Peacemakers in a Nuclear Age," Part I, *Christianity Today,* February 8, 1980, p. 44.
3. Ibid., p. 44.
4. Peter C. Craigie, *The Problem of War in the Old Testament,* p. 94.
5. *Osward Spengler, The Decline of the West,* 2 vols. (New York: Knopf, 1945).
6. R. E. McMasters, "As War Threatens, We Need a Thinking Revolution," *Christian Life,* July 1980, p. 26.
7. Ibid.
8. Lewis W. Walt, *The Eleventh Hour* (Ottawa, IL and Thornwood, NY: Caroline, 1979), p. 3.

CHAPTER
ELEVEN

A Prayer for Peace

Dear Father, whom we cannot see,
   We know that Thou art near;
With longing hearts we turn to Thee,
And ask that Thou wilt set us free
   From war and hate and fear.

Dear Father, King of love and peace,
   We know that Thou art strong;
Make conflicts everywhere to cease,
Let mercy everywhere increase,
   And kindness conquer wrong.

Dear Father, Lord of sea and land,
   We know that Thou art wise;
Oh, make the nations understand
That only by Thy guiding hand
   Can splendid peace arise.

John Oxenham

DOES GOD HAVE
A PLAN FOR AMERICA?

DURING THE CLOSE of the last century, a very strange form of Bible interpretation originated. Today there are still a number of followers of that approach both in the United States and in Great Britain. This system of interpretation, called "Anglo-Israelism" or "British Israelism," teaches that the ten tribes of the Northern Kingdom of Israel, carried away during the Assyrian conquest, later escaped from that country, wandered to Europe, and settled in the British Isles. Thus, the British people, according to this viewpoint, are the true Israelites, and all the blessings that Israel had in the Old Testament now belong to Britain and the United States. America is included because our roots are predominantly British, and that makes the United States a branch of Israel in this very intricate interpretation.

The British Israelites make another emphatic point. They separate Jews and Israelites. According to this idea, the Jews are the descendants of Judah, and they were the only tribe in Palestine during our Lord's ministry on earth. They alone were responsible for the crucifixion of Christ, and a curse has rested on them ever since.

Louis Talbot, a Bible scholar who studied British Israelism said, "I have come to the conclusion that this whole system is a delusion of Satan. It is a denial of the redemptive work of the Lord Jesus Christ, a presentation of a false Messiah, leading people to rest on their national connection for their salvation instead of on the blood of the Lord Jesus."

Many who have strong patriotic feelings or who deliver patriotic messages come close to British Israelism. Using Old Testament passages referring to God's plan for Israel, the patriotic preachers make unwarranted interpretations and applications to the United States. There is much we can learn from the Old Testament, but we do it a great disservice, no matter how zealous our patriotism, when we take its Jewish promises and apply them to America in general and the church in particular.

AMERICA IN SCRIPTURE

The fact is that the United States is not mentioned in the Bible at all. Some have tried to make the United States a secondary part of the analogy of the European Common Market, apparently alluded to in the Book of Daniel. They say that most Americans come from one of the nations in the ten-kingdom federation. Therefore, the prophecies that have to do with the ten nations of the European Market include the United States.

Still others have said that there is no reference to America in the Bible because by the time of the prophetic events of Scripture, she will have ceased to be an important power in the world, or even more frightening, she may have ceased to be altogether. That's a sobering thought!

Yet, as we look in retrospect at the blessing of God upon our young nation, we cannot help but wonder, "Does God have a plan for America?" Peter Marshall and David Manuel ask that question in the introduction to a book that investigates the possibility of God's special involvement with our country:

> What if Columbus' discovering of America had not been accidental at all? What if it were merely the opening curtain of an extraordinary drama? Did God have a special plan for America? Like all those who have discovered the reality of the living Christ, we knew that God had a plan for each individual's life—a plan which could with spiritual effort, be discovered and followed. What if he dealt with whole nations like he dealt with individuals? What if in particular he had a plan for those he would bring to America, a plan which saw this continent as a stage for a new era in the drama of mankind's redemption? Was our vast divergence from this blueprint, after such a promising beginning, the reason why God seemed to be allowing us to move into a new dark age?[1]

A HISTORICAL PERSPECTIVE

Those who study history and the Bible cannot help but notice that there seems to be, as one looks at it from the vantage point of the twentieth century, a very definite indication that God *does* have a plan for America. That we do not have any direct reference to it in the Old or New Testament does not discount the fact that in His sovereign purpose, God could have included America as part of His overall redemptive plan.

A glance at our history will prove that America is no accident. In *The Light and the Glory*, Peter Marshall tells of God's superintending hand upon the life of Christopher Columbus. This adventurer discovered the "New World" by accident, but *not* by accident. God had His hand upon the wheel of the ship and brought it here, even though Columbus himself did not know what was happening. George Washington summarized this thought when he said, "No people can be bound to acknowledge and adore the invisible hand which conducts the affairs of man more than those of the United States."

Someone has written that as you look on this land from history's perspective, you see Washington kneeling in the snow of Valley Forge. You see our Founding Fathers on their knees at the first Continental Congress. You see the gaunt Lincoln praying in the hour of crisis. You see Woodrow Wilson reading his Bible by the White House lights. You see Dwight Eisenhower concluding his inaugural address with a fervent prayer for divine strength and guidance. No, America did not become the land of the free and the home of the brave by blind fate or a happy set of circumstances. A benevolent God was hovering over this nation from her very conception.

One man has written this analogy to help us understand why America is great and why her greatness stands today in jeopardy:

If continental expanse made a nation great, *Siberia* would be the mightiest country. If concentrated population makes a nation great, *India* would be the greatest nation. If ancient culture made a nation great, *China* would be the leader of all the families on earth. What makes a nation great? It is the character of the people. A nation is made not by its fruitful acres, but by the men who till them: not by its rich mines, but by the men who work them.

As Lyman Abbott said, "America was a great *land* when Columbus discovered it; Americans have made it a great *nation*." Look only at her accomplishments in the material realm and you will see God's benevolence. Although America has only 6 percent of the world's population, more than 50 percent of the modern luxuries that characterize civilization are found in this land.

REASONS FOR GOD'S BLESSINGS

Looking at America from our twentieth-century vantage point, we have to ask this question: "Why has God allowed this land to be blessed above all other lands? Why has America in just two hundred plus years outstripped all the ancient and modern civilizations?"

First, America has been blessed by God because she has been the launching pad for the greatest missionary movement in history. To the United States belongs the distinction of providing three-fourths of the missionaries of the last century, and approximately the same amount of money and material aid. The cause of world missions has, therefore, been a major endeavor of the people of America and may do much to explain the blessing God has showered upon our country. If you survey the whole lost and needy world, 75 percent of the missionaries have come from a country boasting only 6 percent of the total world population.

Second, America has been blessed by God because she has been a homeland for the Jewish people and a friend to Jews everywhere. As early as 1970, over 6 million Jews had been protected from harrassment and anti-Semitism in the United States. They have been granted the opportunity for economic, educational, and cultural advancement without fear of losing their religious freedom. Jewish people have always been special to the United States of America. Earlier in this book, a whole chapter was devoted to America's relationship with Israel. It is enough to say here that in keeping with Genesis

12:1-3, we have been blessed as those who have blessed the Jews.

Third, America has been blessed because she has been a laboratory for the development of the principles of freedom. As I have studied both the Old and New Testaments, I have observed that the principles of freedom are united with the tenets of Christianity. This connection is stated most simply in the phrase, "If you know the truth, the truth shall make you free." And America today is the laboratory where those princi-ɔles of freedom can grow and develop and be an example to all the world.

In 1975, the Freedom House made a survey that showed that fewer than one in five people in the world live in freedom. This late in history, 44.9 percent of the world's population is not free in its society, and only 35.3 percent is partly free.[2]

Our freedoms defy the understanding of the rest of the world. Daniel Webster once said, "Liberty exists in proportion to wholesome restraint." And only America has been able to understand that principle and thus make possible the continued existence of liberty. America has learned that liberty without law is anarchy, liberty against law is rebellion, but liberty limited by law is the cornerstone of civilization. America has become the paradise of human liberty. It is a dramatic exclamation point in world history. America stands today as a great oasis in the midst of a troubled, suffering, and enslaved world. America has been blessed by God, because America has been a laboratory for the development of the principles of freedom.

Fourth, America has been blessed by God because America has honored God and His Word. George Washington ennobled the office of the presidency when he said, "It is impossible to rightly govern the world without God and the Bible." Abraham Lincoln agreed: "I believe the Bible is the best gift God has ever given to man. All the good from the Savior of the world is communicated from this Book."

Daniel Webster wrote, "If there is anything in my life that I can remember that has made me a success, it was the early instilling of the Scripture from my parents into my heart." President Grant added, "The Bible is the sheet anchor of our liberties."

In 1835, Alexis de Tocqueville visited our land looking for the cause of her greatness. His written statement clearly assesses this fourth reason for God's blessing upon our country:

I sought for the greatness and genius of America in her commodious harbors and ample rivers, and it was not there. Not until I went into the churches of America and heard her pulpits aflame with righteousness did I understand the secret of her genius and power. . . . America is great because she is good, and if America ever ceases to be good, she will cease to be great.

An unknown poet arrived at this same conclusion:

What makes a nation great,
Not serried ranks and flags unfurled,
Not armored ships that gird the world,
Not hoarded wealth nor busy mills,
Nor cattle on a thousand hills,
Not sages wise, nor schools, nor laws,
Not boasted deeds and freedom's cause,
All these may be, and yet,
The state in the eye of God be far from great.

That land is great which knows the Lord,
Whose songs are guided by His Word;
Where justice rules twixt man and man,
Where love controls an ardent plan;
Where, breathing in His native air,
Each soul finds joy in praise and prayer . . .
Thus may our country, good and great,
Be God's delight . . . man's best estate.

But America today faces a dangerous situation. That danger lies in the departure of this great country from those values and principles that have secured her greatness. Something is happening in this country that has even the most optimistic American concerned:

In the years since Viet Nam, the United States has accumulated a few sorrows that, if not worthy of Job, are at least chastening. A deepening recession is closing automobile plants; unemployment has gone to 7.8%. Inflation has subverted the traditional apparatus of American hope and self-improvement. . . . The nation's allies have developed the habit of treating it with public condescension and private contempt. . . . An uneasy suspicion has formed that the U.S. is about to leave the interstate highway it has cruised along for more than a generation, and return to a two-lane blacktop.[3]

Columnist Jack Anderson sees the same picture:

> Washington—we have been rocked by one news shock after another until our confidence in America has been shaken. . . . The Russians have defied us in Cuba and Afghanistan. Their puppet, Fidel Castro, has sent expeditionary forces to install hostile governments in Angola, Ethiopia and South Yemen, threatening our oil routes. Our own allies have balked at U.S. leadership and have undercut the U.S. economy with their aggressive trade. There is a recession at home . . . galloping inflation, racial strife in America has not healed, the Abscam disclosure provide dismaying evidence that political corruption didn't end with Watergate.[4]

One writer has written that America's problem is that she is rolling in luxury, reveling in excesses, rollicking in pleasure, reeling in drunkenness, revolting in morals, and rotting in sin. America has rejected the God of her youth and has raised up in His place the idols made with her own hands.

LEARNING FROM SCRIPTURE

There are many illustrations in Scripture that warn us that even a long-suffering God will not forever strive with men. If we ignore divine directives, we cannot enjoy God's blessing.

The Book of Judges is a twenty-one-chapter reminder that God will not be mocked. The four-fold cycle so common in Israel's history occurs repeatedly. Rebellion, retribution, repentance, and restoration recycle thirteen times in that brief period of Israel's life. The nation stubbornly refused to learn.

Years later, following the nation's separation into two kingdoms, the same routine was still being repeated. In Judah, Josiah was king. Jeremiah was God's prophet. He had been called by God to warn Jerusalem of her impending judgment. As we follow the rhetoric of Jeremiah, we discover some amazing parallels.

A Glorious Beginning

"Moreover, the word of the Lord came to me, saying, Go and cry in the ears of Jerusalem, saying, Thus saith the Lord; I remember thee, the kindness of thy youth, the love of thine espousals, when thou wentest after me in the wilderness, in a land that was not sown" (Jer. 2:1, 2).

Jeremiah was instructed to remind Judah of her glorious beginning. He told the people to review the unique way in which God had helped them in the barren land of their beginning as an independent nation. Those early days of simple faith and tender relationship to God parallel the earliest days of our nation's history.

Notice in verse three that God was also devoted to Israel: "Israel was holiness unto the Lord, and the firstfruits of his increase: all that devour him shall offend; evil shall come upon them, saith the Lord" (Jer. 2:3).

When Israel was "holiness unto the Lord," set apart unto God, God was devoted to Israel. The psalmist summarized this consistent scriptural theme: "Blessed is the nation whose God is the Lord; and the people he hath chosen for his own inheritance" (Ps. 33:12).

Rebellion

At the beginning of 2:5, Jeremiah referred to Israel's rebellion: "Hear ye the word of the Lord, O house of Jacob, and all the families of the house of Israel: Thus saith the Lord, What iniquity have your fathers found in me, that they are gone far from me, and have walked after vanity, and are become vain?" (Jer. 2:4,5).

The prophet used the rhetorical question to score their hearts. It is as if God was saying to the people of Judah, "What have I done to cause you to rebel against Me?" "What have you seen in Me," asked God, "that caused you to return to your old ways and withhold honor from Me?" Certainly God must be asking that question of our land as well. Perhaps instead of "In God we trust," we should print the words of Psalm 9:17 on our next issue of currency: "The wicked shall be turned into hell, and all the nations that forget God."

Indifference

"Neither said they, Where is the Lord that brought us up out of the land of Egypt, that led us through the wilderness, through a land of deserts and of pits, through a land of drought, and of the shadow of death, through a land that no man passed through, and where no man dwelt?" (Jer. 2:6).

As the message of God's blessing upon Israel was communicated, there was no response by the people. "Neither said they . . ." They were indifferent both to God's blessing and to the prophet's reminder. Their attitude was "So what!" That attitude was exactly what Moses had warned against:

> And it shall be, when the Lord thy God shall have brought thee into the land which he sware unto thy fathers, to Abraham, to Isaac, and to Jacob, to give thee great and goodly cities, *which thou buildest not,* And houses full of all good things, which *thou filledst not,* and wells digged, which thou diggest not, vineyards and olive trees, which *thou plantest not;* when thou shalt have eaten and be full; Then beware lest thou forget *the Lord, which brought thee forth* out of the land of Egypt, from the house of bondage (Deut. 6:10-12, emphasis added).

The indifferent attitude of the Israelites is not unlike the humanistic spirit in our country. We have figured out a way to program God out of our schools, our government, our homes, and even our churches. We do it all in the name of progress. Arthur Guiterman, in *Gaily the Troubadour,* describes this "progress."

> First, dentistry was painless;
> Then bicycles were chainless
> And carriages were horseless
> And many laws, enforceless.
>
> Next, cookery was fireless,
> Telegraphy was wireless,
> Cigars were nicotineless
> And coffee, caffeinless.
>
> Soon oranges were seedless,
> The putting green was weedless,
> The college boy was hatless,
> The proper diet fatless.
>
> Now, motor roads are dustless,
> The latest steel is rustless,
> Our tennis courts are sodless,
> Our new religion's godless.[5]

Spiritual Vacuum

Jeremiah's diagnosis of his nation's woes next extended to the spiritual leadership of his day: "The priests said not, Where is the Lord? and they that handle the law knew me not: the pastors also transgressed against me, and the prophets prophesied by Baal, and walked after things that do not profit" (Jer. 2:8).

Rebellion and indifference filled the pews of Jeremiah's day because there was no voice in the pulpit, no one standing behind the sacred desk, raising a voice for God against sin. Like our liberal preachers, they offered their dying generation empty words of hope, positive thinking instead of the preaching of judgment.

I recently reread *The Church at the End of the Twentieth Century,* written by Francis Schaeffer. In this book, Dr. Schaeffer, one of the foremost conservative theologians of our day, talks about the problem of liberalism in our country.

> This spiritual adultery is worse, much worse, than physical adultery. But it is also much worse, let me say, than the Jews following their idols. Oh, how God spoke out against the Jews following their idols. What strong figures of speech he used in following after them to bring them to their senses! But modern liberal theology is far worse than this. For, it turns against greater light, against greater blessing.[6]

Schaeffer says that modern liberal theology is worse than following the Molech of the Old Testament. Molech was a heathen god whose idol was in the Valley of Hinnom. The followers of Molech sacrificed their children by causing them to pass through fire.

According to tradition, the firstborn of every woman was a required sacrifice to Molech. The idol of Molech was built with an opening in the back. After a fire was made within it, each father had to come and with his own hands place his firstborn in the white-hot, outstretched hands of Molech. The parent was not allowed to show any emotion, and the loud noise of drumbeat was used to cover the cries of the infant as he died in the hands of Molech.

And Schaeffer says:

And there, I would say, stand many in our day. Many of those who come to me, or those with whom I work are the children destroyed by worse than a Molech. Men, who supposedly were the men of God, have stood by while their children were eaten up by modern theology. And then, we are told that there's supposed to be no emotion shown. Some of you who read this bear yourselves the mark of these things from the background from which you have come. All of us are marked by this in some way, to some extent, because our western post-Christian world has been undercut by this liberal theology.

Every scar the present generation has, every tear cried, every baby which some of you who read this have willfully aborted, every drug trip you have taken, cannot be separated from the fact that *the Church* has turned away and become unfaithful. This generation is the generation of babies in the hands of Molech. And are we, as mere puppets, supposed to stand by and hear the cries and cover them by beating loudly the drums of a profitless discussion? I tell you, no! We are to weep and we're to act.[7]

Understand Schaeffer! He says that a liberal theologian who stands before the people of his or her church and fails to declare the Word of God is sacrificing the children of his or her congregation. I would not want to stand in the place of such a person when he or she appears before a righteous God.

These children of liberal theology have become the core of our present humanistic, amoral society. They have grown up not knowing the difference between right and wrong. They have been nurtured on the philosophy of free love and the new morality. They have been told by their spiritual leaders that pornography is adult entertainment, abortion is the right of every woman, and homosexuality is just an alternate life-style. When this is the message coming from the "spiritual leaders" of the day, it is no wonder that judgment is knocking at the door of our nation.

Jeremiah pictured this spiritual vacuum in these graphic terms: "My people have committed two evils; they have forsaken me the fountain of living waters, and hewed them out cisterns, broken cisterns, that can hold no water" (Jer. 2:13).

A cistern at best could furnish only water drained off dirty roofs, and the water was often stagnant from standing in the reservoir. God was saying through the prophet that the people of Israel had two basic problems. They had rejected Him, the fountain of life, and in His place they had substituted the stagnant pools of the world's cheap substitutes—sex, pleasure, intellectualism, materialism, etc.

There Is Still Hope

"Wherefore, I will yet plead with you, saith the Lord, and with your children's children will I plead" (Jer. 2:9). Just as God pled with Jeremiah's generation, I believe He is pleading with our land today. The problems we are facing both internally and internationally are reminding thoughtful Americans that we are not immune to the judgment that has fallen on other God-rejecting nations.

God gave Israel a plan for recovering if they would but listen: "Thus saith the Lord, Stand ye in the ways, and see, and ask for the old paths, where is the good way, and walk therein, and ye shall find rest for your souls" (Jer. 6:15).

The warnings were clear, the plan for recovery was explicit, but for Israel it was too late. She had passed the point of no return. She had become so desensitized to her sin that she no longer felt any shame, and "neither could they blush" (Jer. 6:15). She refused to listen to God's message—"We will not hearken" (Jer. 6:17)—and she refused to change direction— "We will not walk therein" (Jer. 6:16).

And so in 586 b.c., Jerusalem fell and the inhabitants, with the exception of a small remnant, were carried off to Babylon in captivity.

As I have studied the nation of Israel during Jeremiah's ministry, I have not been able to escape the picture of our United States superimposed on this Old Testament passage. No, America is *not* God's modern chosen people. But God has not changed His mind about holiness, righteousness, sin, and judgment. As one man said, "If God does not judge America, He will have to apologize to Sodom and Gomorrah."

When the barbarians, the Vandals, entered Rome, I am told that they listened to an orator in the Senate proposing a plan to stop them if they should ever invade the land. One historian wrote that some of the invaders poked the Roman senators to see if they were alive, for they sat like statues listening to a message of warning against the enemy, while the enemy sat in their midst.

What happened to Israel and to Rome could happen to us if, as Schaeffer suggests, we do not "weep and act." Now is the time for America to recover her greatness by returning to the old paths and the good ways. It is my responsibility and yours to do our part in this renewal. If we do not speak soon it may be too late. Let these words of Martin Niemoller cement the importance of your involvement in your heart and mind:

> In Germany they came first for the Communist, and I didn't speak up because I wasn't a Communist. Then they came for the Jews, and I didn't speak up because I wasn't a Jew. Then they came for the trade unionists, and I didn't speak up because I wasn't a trade unionist. Then they came for the Catholics, and I didn't speak up because I was a Protestant. Then they came for me, and by that time, no one was left to speak up.

NOTES

1. Peter Marshall and David Manuel, *The Light and the Glory* (Old Tappan, NJ: Revell, 1977), pp. 17, 18.
2. Freedom House
3. *Time Magazine,* July 7, 1980.
4. *Washington Post,* July 4, 1980. © 1980 United Feature Syndicate, Inc.
5. Quoted by John Warwick Montgomery, *The Shaping of America* (Minneapolis: Bethany Fellowship, 1976), p. 93.
6. Francis Schaeffer, *The Church at the End of the Twentieth Century* (Downers Grove, IL: InterVarsity, 1979).
7. Ibid.

CHAPTER
TWELVE   *Preach the Word*

Shall I, for fear of mortal man,
The Spirit's course in me restrain?
Or, undismayed, in deed and word
Be a true witness of my Lord?

Awed by a mortal's frown, shall I
Conceal the Word of God most high?
How then before Thee shall I dare
To stand, or how Thine anger bear?

Shall I, to soothe the unholy throng
Soften Thy truths, and smooth my tongue?
To gain earth's gilded toys, or flee
The Cross, endured my Lord, by Thee?

What then is he whose scorn I dread,
Whose wrath or hate makes me afraid?
A man! an heir of death, a slave
To sin! a bubble on the wave!

Yea! let men rage, since Thou wilt spread
Thy shadowing wings about my head;
Since in all pain Thy tender love
Will still my sure refreshment prove.

Give me Thy strength, O God of power;
Then let winds blow or tempests roar;
Thy faithful witness will I be;
'Tis fixed; I can do all through Thee.

Charles Wesley

BEFORE IT'S TOO LATE!

ALMOST TWO HUNDRED years ago, Professor Alexander Tyler wrote the following words about the fall of the Athenian Republic over two thousand years earlier:

> A democracy cannot exist as a permanent form of government. It can only exist until the voters discover that they can vote themselves money from the public treasury. From that moment on, the majority always votes for the candidates promising the most money from the public treasury, with the result that a democracy always collapses over loose fiscal policy, always followed by dictatorship.

> The average age of the world's great civilizations has been 200 years. These nations have progressed through the following sequence: From bondage to spiritual faith, from spiritual faith to great courage, from courage to liberty, from liberty to abundance, from abundance to selfishness, from selfishness to complacency, from complacency to apathy, from apathy to dependency and from dependency back to bondage.

If Tyler is correct in his assessment, America is living on borrowed time. We are already in the complacency to apathy stage and are moving toward dependency. Is it too late for our country?

Let me answer that question by taking you back to a period of Israel's history that is very similar to our own situation today. It was as dark an hour in Judah as it is today in our land. For fifty-five years, Manasseh had been on the throne reaching an all-time low as a monarch. His godless and impenitent son Amon followed him as king and surpassed him in evil. Amon was so wicked that one of his own slaves conspired against him and slew him in his own home. God's judgment was about to fall on that nation when something happened.

Amon's young son Josiah came to the throne. Surrounded by the accumulated evils of his father and grandfather, Josiah led one of the greatest revivals of all time. This young king began to reign at age eight and died at the age of thirty-nine.

J. G. Greenhough describes the uniqueness of Josiah in comparison to the other kings of Israel.

> Four-fifths of them were equally deficient in brains and morals, a combination of wickedness and folly, with nothing of the king about them but the name. But here and there you come upon a man amidst all these royal puppets. It is like finding a garden in a Sahara, or a jewel in a heap of sham trinkets and dirty stage finery. Josiah breaks a long, monotonous series of absolutely worthless monarchs. Before and behind him are moral waste and darkness. He stands out as a figure worth looking at and loving. . . . Josiah's good reign was like a burst of brilliant sunset, before the final darkness comes on.[1]

Second Chronicles 34 tells us that in the eighth year of Josiah's reign, he began to seek after God, and in the twelfth year, he started to purge Judah and Jerusalem of the idols in the land.

What happened in Josiah's day is one of the most remarkable spiritual turnabouts the world has ever seen. The national revival got its start from an unusual set of circumstances. Josiah was concerned about the terrible condition of Solomon's temple, and he undertook to have it refurbished and rebuilt. In the process of renovating the temple, a priest by the name of Hilkiah found a copy of the Book of the Law, what we would call the Bible. Hilkiah took the Book of the Law to Shaphan, the scribe, and he in turn took the Scriptures to King Josiah. The Old Testament Book of Kings records what happened:

> Shaphan the scribe showed the king, saying, Hilkiah the priest hath delivered me a book. And Shaphan read it before the king. And it came to pass, when the king had heard the words of the book of the law, that he rent his clothes (2 Kings 22:10, 11).

Mark well what happened. A man came to the leadership of the nation who determined to seek after God with all his heart.

There never was a better illustration of our Lord's great New Testament principle that he who does the will of God shall know the doctrine of God. (In other words, we learn more about God as we obey what we already know of His will.) For it was in the progress of Josiah's seeking after God that the long-lost law of Moses was recovered. More than one scholar has observed that apart from Josiah's tender and seeking heart, we might not have the books of Moses today. But let's go on. As King Josiah was exposed to God's Word, he led his people in a vow to follow obediently the commands of God:

And the king stood by a pillar, and made a covenant before the Lord, to walk after the Lord, and to keep his commandments and his testimonies and his statutes with all their heart and all their soul, to perform the words of this covenant that were written in this book. And all the people stood to the covenant (2 Kings 23:3).

Can you imagine the effect of such a covenant upon the national life of Judah? Can you dare to dream what would happen in America if just God's own people were to sign such a covenant of obedience to His Word?

And 2 Kings 23 tells us further that King Josiah reinstituted the Passover and that the Passover during the days of Josiah's reign was the greatest of all the days of Israel's history: "Surely there was not holden such a passover from the days of the judges who judged Israel, nor in all the days of the kings of Israel, nor of the kings of Judah" (2 Kings 23:22).

While King Josiah was leading the revival from a political aspect, he was being assisted by the great prophet Jeremiah. For eighteen years the voice of the weeping prophet thundered righteousness throughout the land. He was joined later by the prophets Zephaniah and Nahum.

When King Josiah was in his early twenties, he set about a national reformation of religion as radical and complete as anything that Martin Luther, John Calvin, or John Knox ever undertook. Idolatry was destroyed, and homosexuality was obliterated. The idolatrous priests were slain, and the medi-

ums, wizards, images, and idols were all searched out and
destroyed.

During this same period in Judah's history, God raised up
Daniel and his three friends, Hananiah, Azariah, and Meshael.
I am convinced that their exposure to Josiah and Jeremiah
shaped their lives so that they would be ready later to stand
alone for God in the midst of a perverted Chaldean culture.

What elements stand out in the renewal of Judah? They are
so obvious that you've no doubt already picked out the following points.

1. A Spiritual Person

God always begins with a person. The Bible simply says that
"Josiah did that which was right in the sight of the Lord"
(2 Kings 22:2), and "He walked in the ways of David his father,
and declined neither to the right hand, nor to the left" (2 Chr.
34:2).

Writing about another period in Israel's history, Leonard
Ravenhill says:

> How the God of glory had departed! The salt had lost its savour!
> The gold had become dim! But out of this measureless backslid-
> ing, God raised up a *man*—not a committee, not a sect, not an
> angel, but a *man,* and a man of like passions as we are! God
> 'sought for a man', not to preach, but to stand in the gap. As
> Abraham, so now Elijah 'stood before the Lord.' . . . He knew
> the mind of God. Therefore, he—one man—strangled a nation
> and altered the course of nature.[2]

In the Valley of Megiddo, on Josiah's tombstone, is this
tribute to his tender heart and his tough leadership:

> The remembrance of Josiah is like the perfume of the apothe-
> cary, and his name is like music at a banquet of wine. For his
> pure and holy youth, Jehovah was his shield in the hour of
> temptation, till he behaved himself rightly in the conversion
> of his people, and till he took away all their abominations of
> iniquity. He directed his heart to the Lord, and he established
> the worship of God: and all because his heart was so tender. The
> remembrance of Josiah in Judah and in Jerusalem is like the
> perfume of the apothecary, and like music at a banquet of wine.[3]

The Scripture gives its own appraisal of this great man:

And like unto him was there no king before him, that turned to
the Lord with all his heart, and with all his soul, and with all his
might, according to all the law of Moses; neither after him arose
there any like him (2 Kings 23:25).

2. A Spiritual Hunger

"In the eighth year of his reign . . . he began to seek after the
God of David his father" (2 Chr. 34:3). It is important to note
that four years before Josiah began his public work of reformation and cleansing of the nation, he began to seek God. He built
a firm groundwork of personal piety on which to erect the
superstructure of active service. Is it possible that those of us
who are trying to do something to stop the spiritual death of
our country have bypassed this important prerequisite?

The four great spiritual awakenings that have taken place in
our country were fueled by the fervent seeking after God of a
few concerned souls. This is how it happened in the mid-1800s:

In the middle of the nineteenth century, when our nation was
divided over the issue of slavery, and people were living in a
selfish, materialistic approach to life, God raised up Jeremiah
Lamphier to lead a revival of prayer. In 1857, he began a prayer
meeting in the upper room of the Old Fulton Street Dutch
Reform Church in Manhattan. Beginning with only six people,
the prayer meeting grew until the church was filled with praying
people. By February of 1858, nearly ten thousand people a
week were being converted. The impact of these prayer meetings spread from city to city across the United States. Cleve-
land, Detroit, Chicago, Cincinnati—city after city was
conquered by the power of believing prayer.[4]

All the great revivals in other lands have begun exactly the
same way. This was proved some years ago in the Telugu-
speaking area of India. Over two thousand people had been
baptized in a single day. But as time went on, a coldness moved
into the church so that there appeared to be a spiritual death.
Some of the saints became greatly disturbed by the lack of
spiritual power. They banded together in prayer, asking the

Lord to revive His work. After much preparation, ten days were set aside to pray specifically for revival.

A missionary told what happened during one of those meetings. "At about 8:00, at what seemed an ordinary meeting, someone was praying, when suddenly there was a sob. One cried out. Like a flash, something came over the meeting and there was a tumult of sound, cries, groans, and beseeching calls on God. One present said it sounded like a rushing mighty wind." Another missionary said, "For the first time in thirty-three years in India we have really seen natives crying for their sins." This feature much impressed the heathen. They crowded the door, saying, "Why, they are crying for their sins. How strange."[5]

What God did in India, He wants to do in every country of the world. The church today is cold, indifferent, and powerless. If we are to experience revival, there must be a new seeking after God with all our hearts and souls and minds.

3. A Spiritual Book

"Hilkiah the priest hath delivered me a book. . . . And it came to pass, when the king had heard the words of the book of the law, that he rent his clothes" (2 Kings 22:10, 11). Spiritual renewal is inseparably linked to the Word of God. The great renewal during Nehemiah's time was engendered when "all the people gathered themselves together as one man into the street that was before the water gate; and they spoke unto Ezra the scribe to bring the book of the law of Moses, which the Lord had commanded to Israel" (Neh. 8:1).

The reason for the centrality of the Word of God in revival should be obvious. The terrible conditions that faced Josiah resulted from the *neglect* of that book, and it was only as that book was restored to the lives of the people that revival could start:

> Let us remember that all the mischief, all the corruption and confusion, all the shame and dishonor, all the reproach and blasphemy, had its origin in the neglect of the Word of God. . . .
> It has ever been the special design of Satan to lead God's people away from Scripture. He will use anything and everything for this end—tradition—the church, so-called—expediency—

human reason—popular opinion—reputation and influence—character, position, and usefulness—all those he will use in order to get the heart and conscience away from that one golden sentence—that divine motto, "It is written."[6]

This centrality of the Word of God in spiritual renewal is especially noteworthy for two reasons: first, because our "Christian" land is suffering from the death of biblical preaching; and second, because many who have set out to bring America back to God have in the process of their efforts abandoned the very means God has promised to use to accomplish that end.

The words of the prophet Amos seem to be fulfilled in our day:

> Behold, the days come, saith the Lord God, that I will send a famine in the land, not a famine of bread, nor a thirst for water, but of hearing the words of the Lord: And they shall wander from sea to sea, and from the north even to the east; they shall run to and fro to seek the word of the Lord, and shall not find it (Amos 8:11-12).

We have all-night sings, gospel entertainment, puppet shows, carefully choreographed specials, multimedia extravaganzas, forums, expos, explos, seminars, films, and dialogues. But where is the preaching of the Word of the Lord? It has been well said:

> There is a famine of great preaching, a famine of strong expository preaching, a famine of conscience—stirring preaching, a famine of heartbreaking preaching, a famine of soul-tearing preaching, a famine of that preaching like our fathers knew which kept men awake all night lest they fall into hell. I repeat, "There is a famine of the Word of the Lord."[7]

We are told the famous British actor Garrick was once asked by a bishop how it was that he produced far more powerful results by fiction than the bishops could by preaching the truth. The reply of the actor is full of force. "My Lord," he said, "the reason is obvious. I speak fiction as though it were truth, whereas you speak truth as though it were fiction."

Recently a pastor friend of mine was asked to write an article on the phenomenal success of the Basic Youth Conflicts Seminars conducted by Bill Gothard in the major arenas of our land. He went to the week-long seminar as a skeptic, certain that he would find some external and nonspiritual reason for Gothard's success.

On Friday night, after the session was concluded for that day, he called me from his hotel room. "I've got it," he said. "I know what makes it happen!" He then came out with this simple but stinging conclusion: "Bill Gothard is so successful," he said, "because we preachers are so unsuccessful." What a shot! But is there any other way to explain why tens of thousands of Christian people jam into the convention centers of our land to hear what is at best simple Bible truth taught in a very low-key style?

Bill Gothard is simply meeting a need that is not being met in many of the churches of our land. And I do not stand alone when I say that America cannot survive another decade of decline in Bible preaching.

The second concern of my heart is the trend among many good preachers to give up their pulpits for the soapbox. This whole book is about my love for America. It is because of my love for this land that I cannot bear the thought of gifted, spirit-called men of God trading the power of the Word of God for the anemic platitudes of political jargon. This country doesn't need any more political speeches. Our people need to hear "thus saith the Lord."

Should men of God not speak to the issues of our day? Without question they should. You cannot preach the Word of God faithfully and ignore today's issues. The uniqueness of God's message is its timeless application to people's needs. But we must not, from the same pulpit from which we declare God's truth, make statements that go *beyond* revelation. We preachers may have our own firm opinions about issues not addressed in the Bible, but we ought not to confuse ourselves or our parishioners by voicing them from the pulpit or with the same authority used to state God's clear commands.

When the prophet Daniel was nearing the end of his ministry, he was called one night to speak to a thousand drunk politicians and their wicked, profligate king. His responsibility that night was to boldly interpret what God had supernaturally written on the wall of the banquet hall. The message of the evening was not an easy one. He literally announced the end of the Babylonian kingdom. He stood unflinchingly before that group of sinners and without apology declared God's Word to them. Some of the Babylonians may have considered his message political in nature, but Daniel knew he was declaring the authoritative Word of God. What God has written we also may preach with authority.

Joseph Parker reminds us that we, like Daniel, may be called upon in a soon-coming hour:

> Preachers of the Word, you will be wanted someday by Belshazzar; you were not at the beginning of the feast, you will be there before the banquet hall is closed. . . . The king will not ask you to drink wine, but he will ask you to tell the secret of his pain and heal the malady of his heart. Abide your time. You are nobody now. Who cares for preachers, teachers, seers, men of insight, while the wine goes around, and the feast is unfolding its tempting luxuries? But the preacher will have his opportunities. They will send for him when all other friends have failed. May he then come fearlessly, independently asking only to be *a medium through which divine communication can be addressed to the listening trouble of the world* (emphasis added).[8]

4. A Spiritual People

The last five verses of 2 Chronicles 34 demonstrate the impact that a man of God, committed to the Word of God, will have on the people of God:

> Then the king sent and gathered together all the elders of Judah and Jerusalem. And the king went up into the house of the LORD, and all the men of Judah, and the inhabitants of Jerusalem, and the priests, and the Levites, and all the people, great and small: and he read in their ears all the words of the book of the covenant that was found in the house of the LORD. And the king stood in his place, and made a covenant before the LORD, to walk after the LORD, and to keep his commandments, and his testimonies, and his statutes, with all his heart, and with all his

soul, to perform the words of the covenant which are written in this book. And he caused all that were present in Jerusalem and Benjamin to stand to it. And the inhabitants of Jerusalem did according to the covenant of God, the God of their fathers. And Josiah took away all the abominations out of all the countries that pertained to the children of Israel, and made all that were present in Israel to serve, even to serve the LORD their God. And all his days they departed not from following the LORD, the God of their fathers (2 Chr. 34:29-33).

Josiah brought together all the men, *all* the inhabitants of Jerusalem—the priests, the Levites, all the people great and small—and he did three very important things:

1. He read to them all the words of the book of the covenant.
2. He made a personal covenant to follow the instruction of the Word of God himself with all his heart and soul.
3. He caused all his people to stand to it.

The result was that "all his days, they departed not from following the Lord, the God of their fathers."

I agree with much that has been accomplished by the secular moral action groups that have grown up during the last five years. The Coalition for Better Television and the pro-life groups are just two positive examples of human efforts that have raised the moral climate of our nation.

I come back again, however, to the spiritual dimension of renewal and reform. Whenever God addresses the subject of national change, He speaks primarily to His own people. "If *my* people, which are called by *my* name, shall humble *themselves* . . . I . . . will heal their land" (2 Chr. 7:14, emphasis added). Though spoken specifically to Israel, this verse illustrates, I believe, what God longs to do for any nation.

If our leadership begins to seek after God, if the Word of God is restored to its rightful place of authority in our churches, and if Christian people covenant to walk after God in holiness and righteousness, God may yet restore America to health.

Josiah might have considered his cause to be hopeless. He might have thought that nothing could avert the mighty tide of wrath and judgment that was about to cover the city of Jerusalem and the land of Israel. But he did what he could do, and his concerted effort was blessed by a turning of the nation back to God.

Whittier challenges us to do the same before it's too late:

Is the old pilgrim spirit quenched within us?
Stoops the proud manhood of our souls so low;
That mammon's lure or party's wile can win us to silence now?
Now, when our land to ruin's brink is verging,
In God's name let us speak while there is time:
Now, when the padlocks of our lips are forging,
Silence is a crime!

NOTES

1. Quoted by Herbert Lockyer, *All the Men of the Bible* (Grand Rapids, MI: Zondervan, 1979), p. 207.
2. Leonard Ravenhill, *Why Revival Tarries* (Minneapolis: Bethany Press, 1959), p. 38.
3. Alexander Whyte, *Bible Characters,* vol. I (Grand Rapids, MI: Zondervan, 1952), p. 362.
4. Jerry Falwell, *Listen America* (Garden City, N.Y.: Doubleday, 1980), pp. 246, 247.
5. J. Allen Blair, *Living Courageously* (Neptune, NJ: Loizeaux, 1971), p. 124.
6. C. H. MacKintosh, *Life and Times of Josiah* (Denver, CO: Wilson Foundation), pp. 19, 20.
7. Leonard Ravenhill, *America Is Too Young to Die* (Minneapolis: Bethany Press, 1979), p. 79.
8. Joseph Parker, *Preaching Through the Bible,* vol. 16 (Grand Rapids, MI: Baker, 1961), p. 415.